THE FRENCH CONQUEST OF ALGERIA

THE FRENCH CONQUEST OF ALGERIA

BY
MAJOR G. B. LAURIE
ROYAL IRISH RIFLES

The Naval & Military Press Ltd

Published by
The Naval & Military Press Ltd
Unit 10, Ridgewood Industrial Park,
Uckfield, East Sussex,
TN22 5QE England
Tel: +44 (0) 1825 749494
Fax: +44 (0) 1825 765701
www.naval-military-press.com
© The Naval & Military Press Ltd 2004

In reprinting in facsimile from the original, any imperfections are inevitably reproduced and the quality may fall short of modern type and cartographic standards.

PREFACE

In 1887, whilst at Gibraltar, I read in the garrison library there, the 'Diary of a Zouave Officer.' I then tried to obtain a complete history of the Conquest of Algeria, and found that there was none in the English language. After waiting twenty years, and finding that still one had not appeared, I have attempted to write a summary of that Conquest.

I should be sorry to enumerate the books bearing on the subject which I have read, as they have been many. I am particularly indebted to the works of M. Rousset, of Sir Lambert Playfair, of the Duc d'Orleans, and of Colonel Scott.

In particular, I have followed the first in all facts and figures when there has been any divergency of statement.

If M. Rousset's history had been translated into English, there would have been no reason for the appearance of this volume.

My thanks are also due to the gentleman who so kindly helped to prepare my maps.

G. B. L.

ALDERSHOT, 1909.

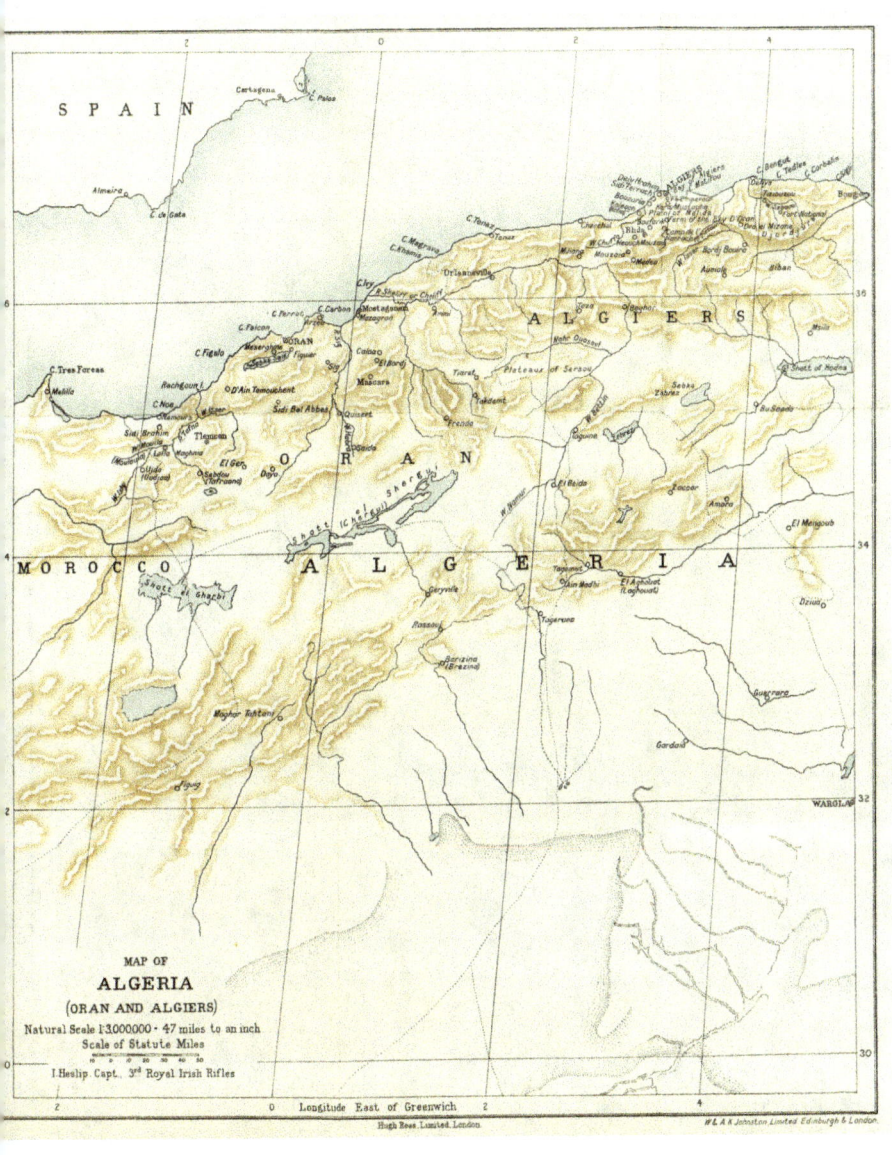

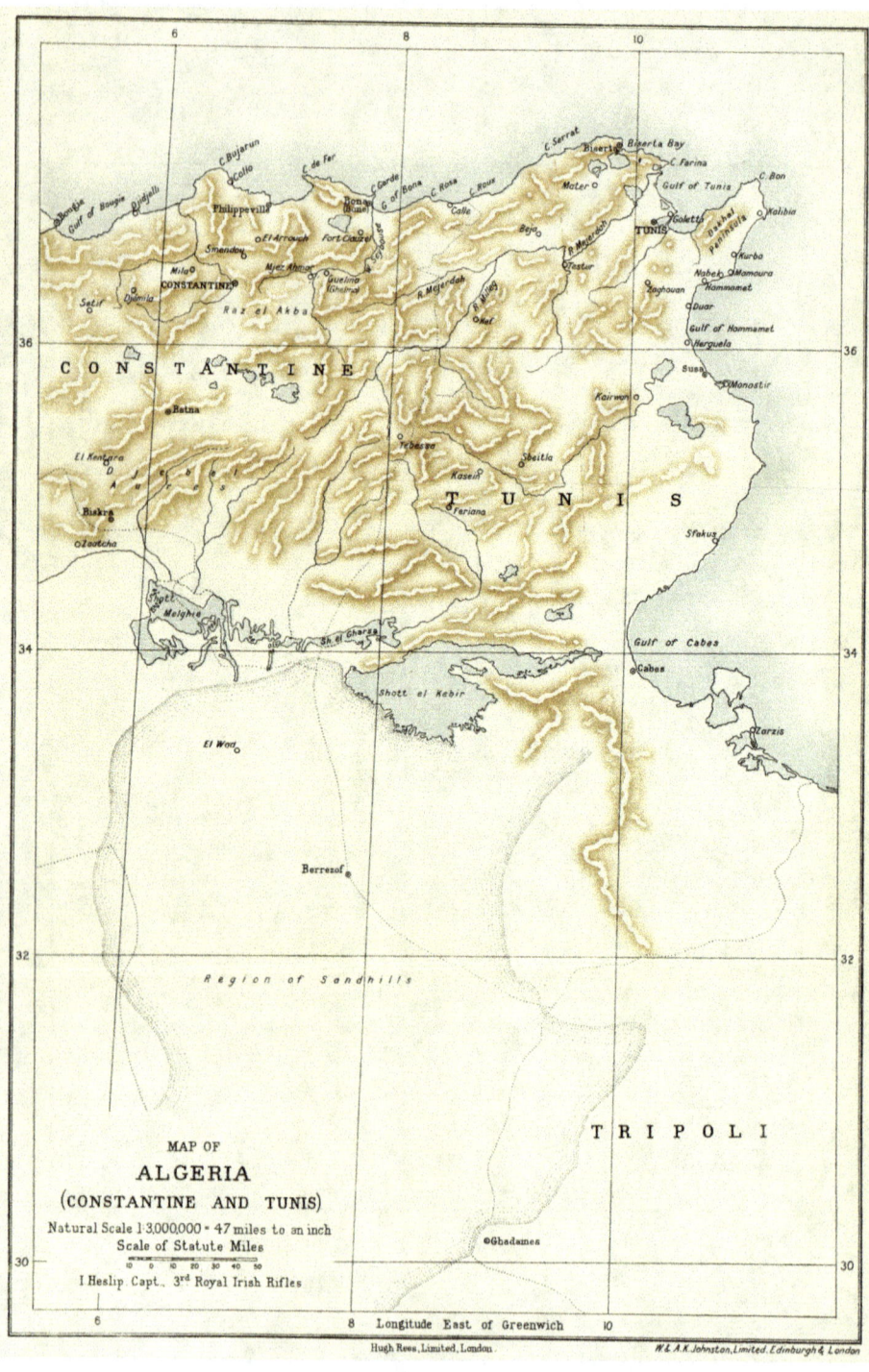

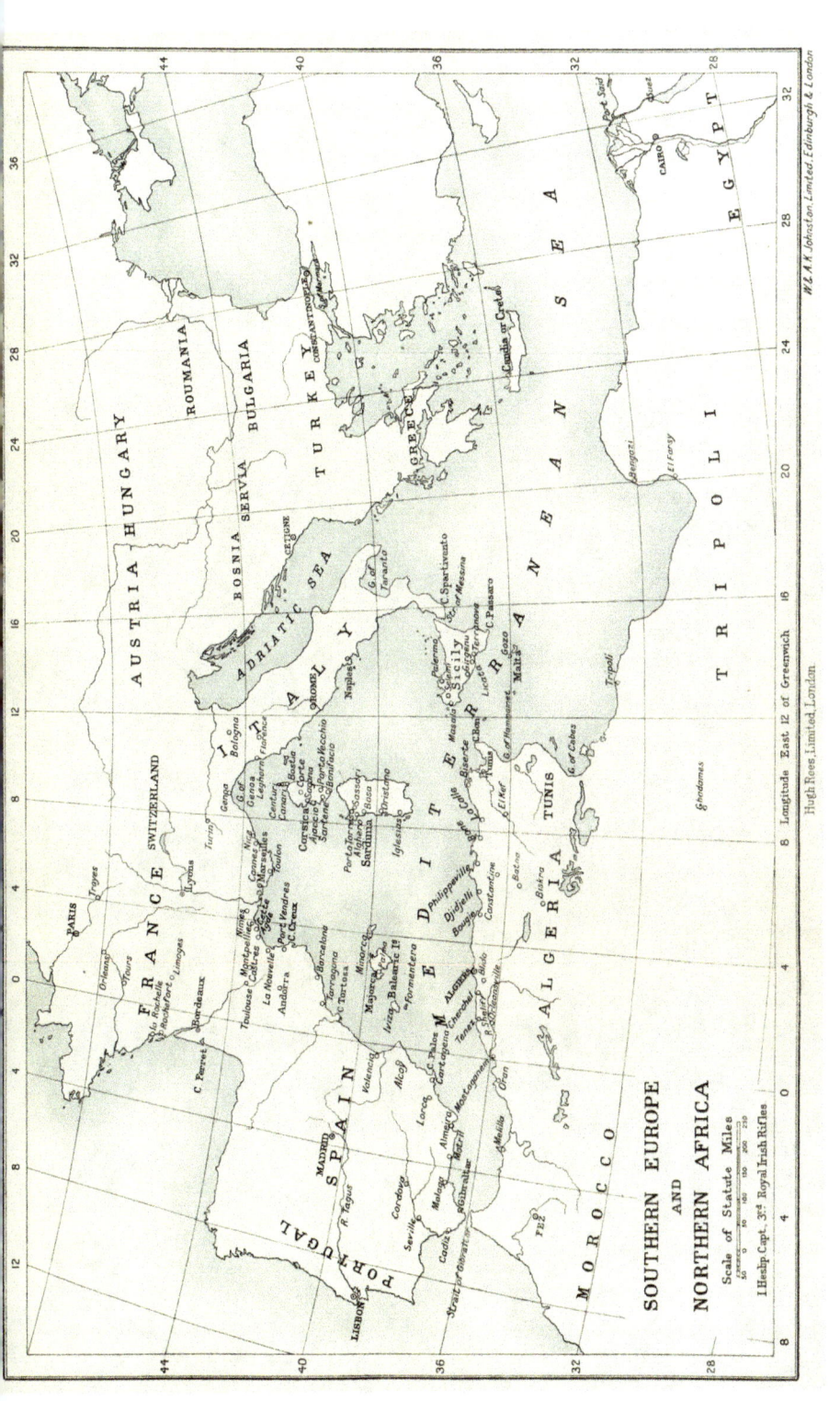

THE CONQUEST OF ALGERIA

CHAPTER I

BEFORE proceeding to describe the Conquest of Algeria by the French, it would perhaps be as well to consider exactly what Algeria consists of, what was its previous history, and what were the reasons that induced the French to proceed to the conquest of this province, which has cost them so dearly in lives and gold.

Algeria is the name now given to the portion of Northern Africa which borders on the Mediterranean Sea, and it is bounded on the west by the semi-barbarous empire of Morocco, on the east by the state of Tunis now under French Government, and to the south it sinks away into the Sahara and French Nigeria.

It stretches for about 550 miles along the coast from east to west, and for nearly 400 miles inland in its widest point.

Algeria is naturally divided into three parts—
(1) The Tell, or Coast Region;
(2) The High Plateaus;
(3) The Sahara Region.

The Tell or Coast Region is very fertile, and was formerly one of the granaries of the Roman Empire, and travellers within the last one hundred and fifty years describe it as covered with ruins of Roman towns, &c.

It is from 75 to 150 miles wide, and it is traversed by seventeen distinct ranges of the Atlas Mountains.

The climate is healthy, excepting just on the coast, where it is rather feverish, as the French found to their cost.

The High Plateaus are broad uplands about 2,500 feet above the sea level.

These plateaus are traversed by the Sahara chains of the Atlas Mountains, of which the loftiest peak is some 7,000 feet high.

The climate is good but trying, as the temperature varies enormously, not only between day and night, but also between the different seasons of the year; as, for instance, in August the thermometer may register 92^0 at night (Fahrenheit), whilst three months later it will be 80^0 less, with snow lying for weeks on the ground.

The Sahara Region consists of wide sandy or rocky plains. Water is generally scarce and the temperature is very high. Rain seldom falls, and life only exists around the oases, or cultivated places, of this desert.

A recent traveller describes the Sahara as a dreadful dreary waste, and states that the heat on the thin layer of sand over the sheets of rocks is sometimes as great as 200^0 (Fahrenheit) during the day in the sun, but before dawn, the temperature will have, perhaps, fallen to below freezing-point (32^0); and he further mentions that the deserts, though in many places resembling the 'dunes' on the northern coast of Prussia, are often simply level wastes of sand, strewn,

THE CONQUEST OF ALGERIA

in some cases, entirely with sharp stones, and in others with rounded smooth ones, as though they had been subject to the action of water. Algeria, of course, does not claim very much of the Sahara. Some idea of the extent of the whole of this awful desert may be gathered, when it is stated, that it is three times the size of the Mediterranean Sea, or ten times the size of Germany. Part of the above tract has, however, a regular though inadequate rainfall. Its extent exceeds 2,500,000 square miles.

It is, fortunately, broken up by some green islands dotted about this sand sea, which islands are, of course, the oases spoken of above. These oases are formed in various ways. Some depend on 'surface' streams, others have underground rivers or springs, from which they draw their supplies. In some cases water is found at a depth of one foot; in others, wells must be sunk fifteen or thirty feet before water is obtained. These oases mark the routes across the Sahara. Caravans of merchants, travellers, columns of troops or raiding bands of Arabs, must all, more or less, come by these places, where, only, water is to be obtained. With these held by garrisons, the roads are blocked at will, and the country behind is in perfect security.

The rivers of Algeria are not navigable, and generally are raging torrents during rain, and dry nullahs or ravines shortly afterwards.

There are but few lakes in Algeria, and those are principally in the desert. They are sometimes of large extent, but are very shallow, and are quickly evaporated. They are usually strongly impregnated with various salts, and are fed by underground springs, which must be very copious, to make up for the constant evaporation under the Algerian sun. When drying up, these lakes form marshes, called by the natives 'sebkhas'; the mud on the surface is apparently firm, but being unwarily stepped upon, allows the traveller to sink into a slimy, swampy bed beneath.

A curious fact about these swamps has been noted, namely, that the mud on the surface almost always contracts into regular polygons, generally of hexagonal shape.

Minerals of all sorts abound in Algeria, with one important exception, and that is, that there is no *coal* in the country.

The country of Algeria is also now divided into three divisions by the French, which, from east to west, are as follows:—Province of Constantine, Province of Algiers, and Province of Oran. The Deys of Algiers, whom the French dispossessed, had a fourth division, called Titteri, which was a stretch of country ruled by a 'bey,' and it was really what we should now call the 'Hinterland' of Algiers, being more or less the southern or inland portion of the present Government of Algiers. Algiers always was the principal town, with a present population of about 120,000 inhabitants, whilst the total population of Algeria at the present time may be put down at 364,000 Europeans and 4,375,000 natives. Despite the heavy fighting which took place during the twenty-seven years that the French occupied in conquering the country, it is probable that the population has largely increased since 1830, the year of the French invasion.

The eastern division of the country had Constantine for the chief city of the Government of Constantine,

THE CONQUEST OF ALGERIA

and seaports called Bougie and Boné, whilst Oran was the chief town of the Government of that name, with inland cities of Tlemcen, Mascara, &c., with other inland towns in the Algiers Government, called Miliana, Blida, Medea, &c.

The native inhabitants of Algeria are by no means a homogeneous people, but are divided into eight distinct classes, of which the following is the list:—

(1) Kabyles or Berbers, they being the original inhabitants of the country. These are a very industrious, independent people, who mostly inhabit the mountains and fertile valleys, and prove themselves quite ready to defend their territory against all comers.

(2) Arabs, who came originally from Asia. Sir Lambert Playfair states that the great Arab immigration occurred about A.D. 1060, and that these Arabs had been conquered in Syria by the Fatimite caliphs, and were banished to Upper Egypt, whence they soon found their way into and overspread all the country between Egypt and the Atlantic Ocean, driving the Berbers into their mountains and taking possession of the plain.

(3) Moors, emigrants from Morocco, and descendants of those expelled from Spain about A.D. 1609.

(4) Jews, principally those expelled from Italy, and also those expelled from Spain about A.D. 1600.

(5) Turks, soldiers and sailors who settled there when Algeria was under the Turkish suzerainty.

(6) Half-bred Turks, called 'Coulouglis,' originally the children of Turkish soldiers and sailors who married the women of the country. Their sons have turned out fine fighting material, something in the same manner as the Cape boys in the southern

extremity of Africa, where they are the descendants of the Dutch and the Kaffir women.

(7) Negroes, descendants of slaves.

(8) The Mozabites, who inhabit the coast towns, and who are quiet and peaceable.

Before turning to the history of Algeria, it is perhaps as well to point out that the mountainous nature of the country has always enabled it to offer a strenuous resistance to permanent invaders when the inhabitants felt so disposed, whilst both ancient and modern conquerors who have had the control of the sea have found it most useful in keeping law and order in force in the coast region, as the valleys running towards the sea can be entered with ease and dispatch from the sea, whilst the tribes in the neighbouring valleys, to support their friends, have to laboriously climb the intervening mountain ranges, and thus they can be defeated in detail. And now to the history of this present French possession. It is a fascinating one, but only on the surface. What life must have been in such a place, say, about A.D. 1700 is hard to imagine; certainly it could not have been wanting in excitement or danger. Still, to make it as short as possible so as to come to the year of the French invasion, namely, A.D. 1830, it may as well be said that the first recorded history of Algeria states that it was occupied by two rival nations, the Massyli and the Massæsyli. In the Punic Wars the former sided with the Romans and the latter with the Carthaginians. At the close of these wars the Roman allies, the Massyli, received the whole country and formed the kingdom of Numidia. In the contest between Pompey and Cæsar, Numidia took Pompey's side,

THE CONQUEST OF ALGERIA 7

and on his final defeat and death it became a Roman province. Remains of Roman roads, aqueducts, camps, and harbours are numerous all over the country. Christianity was early introduced, and flourished exceedingly. About A.D. 430, a Teutonic tribe called Vandals, who had pushed their way into the South of Spain, commenced to make maritime expeditions of a piratical nature. Fired by the success of their voyages, they crossed into Northern Africa under the leadership of Geneseric, and, whilst their ships kept the whole western Mediterranean in terror, the Vandals on land pushed rapidly along the North African coast towards the east, swallowing up the whole of Numidia as well as Carthage, which stood further to the east than Algeria. They had at first been invited to Numidia by the Roman governor Count Boniface, who had been falsely accused of treason to the Roman Emperor, and in self-defence summoned these warriors to his aid A.D. 429. No doubt this conquest was greatly helped by the Berber, or hill tribes, who were not too well affected towards their grasping Roman masters; and it was further helped by the command of the sea, which this race of land warriors had so suddenly acquired. The term 'Vandal' still lives as a sign of an illiterate Boer who destroys all civilisation for the mere pleasure of destruction. It is open to doubt, however, if this tribe really deserved all the hard things said of it. No doubt the native inhabitant was not backward in the work of destruction, as the public buildings and villas, &c., were owned and used by an alien race who had but few common interests with the cultivators of the soil.

Their triumph was, however, of but short duration.

Justinian's great general Belisarius drove them out or destroyed them, some hundred years later, A.D. 533. About the middle of the seventh century, one of Mahomet's followers boldly invaded Egypt, with an army of 8,000 fighting men, and having conquered it, and driven out the Roman owners (who really were the Greeks of the Eastern Empire at Constantinople), spread with the rapidity of a forest fire across the whole of Northern Africa, until they rode their Syrian chargers into the Atlantic on the western shores of Morocco, and called Allah and Mahomet to witness, that there were no countries left for them to conquer for their faith. Numidia fell with the rest of the Roman African possessions, principally, however, through the treachery of the inhabitants; and thus Numidia passed under the rule of the Saracens, and remained for centuries a turbulent, unknown community, sometimes united into one kingdom, sometimes divided into many.

One point about the Mahomedan invasion may be noted, which is, that in A.D. 687 a chieftainess named El Kabina governed one of the strong Berber tribes. She, to resist the Mahomedans, ordered the trees to be cut down from Tripoli to the Atlantic, thus changing the country from a veritable garden to a howling wilderness, from which calamity it has never completely recovered. Bruce, the great traveller, however, notes that in 1770 there were great forests here and there through the country, whilst quite lately Sir Lambert Playfair (in 1875) reports these forests as destroyed by gradual cutting, or by carelessness in letting forest fires run through them unchecked.

About A.D. 1390 the Genoese sent a force to chastise

the Algerians. A large number of this force are said by Froissart to have been English, under Henry IV. of England, at that time Duke of Lancaster. The force landed on the Tunisian coast near Mehedia, where the English archers did good service with their long-bows, beating back the enemy from the shores.

They besieged Mehedia; 'but at length, the scalding air in that hot country breeding in the army sundry diseases, they fell to a compensation and returned home.'

Again, coming to the year 1505, Spain, having driven out the Moorish kings, and having consolidated into one power the present kingdom of Spain, was grasping the new world so recently discovered for her, by Columbus, with one hand, whilst with the other she snatched at various coveted possessions to the east of the Iberian peninsula in a manner which made one think that the vaunting motto of Castile, 'Non sufficint orbis,' was really part of her political faith.

At that time Ferdinand, King of Spain, sent a force under the Count of Navarre, which took Oran and Algiers and the country round them. Barbarossa, the famous Turkish corsair, was then called in to aid Algeria, and having more or less loosened the Spaniard's hold on the country, he then proceeded to murder the native princes and establish himself as king.

Later on, the Spaniards took him prisoner and beheaded him, but his brother rose to the occasion, and after proclaiming himself sultan, placed his kingdom under the protection of the Turks. He is said to have fortified Algiers to an unheard-of extent, employing on the mole about 30,000 Christian slaves for three years.

The Turks in Algiers were now thoroughly embarked on their career as pirates, and they made themselves so obnoxious to their Christian neighbours that in A.D. 1541 Charles the Fifth of Spain attempted the conquest of Algiers and the surrounding country. He took with him an army of 30,000 men, and a fleet of 160 ships. Unfortunately, after landing, a great storm arose and one hundred of his vessels were wrecked. The enemy not unnaturally took advantage of his misfortunes and made a sudden attack upon him, whereby he lost a large part of his army, and he was glad to re-embark the remainder in safety and to depart with all possible speed. It is said that the reason of this defeat of the Spanish troops arose from the fact that they were drenched in a dreadful rain for forty-eight hours, and that when they were attacked by the Turks from Algiers, their firearms could not be discharged. This appears to be a probable explanation, as these troops of Charles the Fifth were veterans, and the flower of his army, consisting of Germans, Italians, and Spaniards.

The emperor was the last to embark in this retreat, and throughout he was urged to renew the fight by 'Cortes,' famous as the conqueror of Mexico, as this hardy warrior was well aware how small were the forces opposed to them.

In A.D. 1609 the Spanish Government saw fit to expel the descendants of the Moors who still remained in Spain. These unfortunate people went naturally to their co-religionists in Northern Africa, and their arrival supplied plenty of recruits to the Turks in Algiers, who continued their piratical cruises with increased vigour.

THE CONQUEST OF ALGERIA

During the seventeenth century several attacks were made on Algiers by the French, English, and Venetians, the most formidable being in A.D. 1683 by the French. Most of the town of Algiers was burnt by the fire of the French fleet on this occasion, and all the French residents were murdered in retaliation by order of the Dey. The French consul in particular was tied to a mortar and blown out to the French flagship. Despite all these unfortunate checks, the pirates flourished amazingly. Their swift cruisers, being generally manned by rowers as well as being provided with sails, were capable of overhauling most of the small merchantmen in the Mediterranean, whilst they even ventured into the English Channel. In proof of how venturesome these pirates were and what voyages they undertook, it is worth mentioning that during, or about, the time of the Civil War in England in the reign of Charles the First, a clergyman relates that he embarked at Youghal for England with six or seven other passengers, and that he was captured, within sight of Ireland the same day, by an 'Algire Piratt,' who put the men in stocks and chains, and duly carried them to Algiers. During the eighteenth century, however, they appear to have left the English commerce severely alone.

So long as England was at war with France and Spain, as she was off and on from A.D. 1690 to 1815, it was unstatesmanlike to raise up a further enemy on the Mediterranean coast, and she, in common with all the other nations, paid an annual allowance to these pirates as 'blackmail,' so that their ships might be left in peace. But when continental matters were finally settled so far as Britain was concerned after A.D. 1815, it was thought full time to give these sea robbers a much-needed lesson. So in A.D. 1816 a British fleet was sent to Algiers to present a demand that all Christian slaves should be released. It consisted of five ships of the line and some frigates, and was joined at Gibraltar by six Dutch frigates, whose commander asked as a special favour that he might be allowed to take part if any fighting should occur. The British demand was treated with contempt, and the guns of the town opened fire on the fleet. All the shore batteries and all the shipping in harbour were then destroyed by the broadsides of the line of battle ships. The forts opposed to the British fleet mounted in all some 520 guns.

The lesson was sufficient for the time, and next day all the Christian slaves were released, to the number of 3,003. The British loss was over 500 killed and wounded in this evening's fighting, whilst the enemy lost 7,000.

It should perhaps be added that the iniquity, which finally drove the English Government to inflict this punishment on these barbarians, was the massacre of the unarmed crews of the coral fishing boats at Boné. These poor creatures had gone on shore as usual to attend Mass, it being Ascension Day, and they were promptly set upon by a numerous body of armed Turks and were all murdered.

We now come to the period which this book proposes to describe; but before that is entered upon, it will be well to see something of the internal history of this nest of thieves. Their idea of government is perhaps best illustrated by a few old extracts from papers on the treatment of their slaves, whilst the recital of the reigns of the last two or three Deys will show what a volcano they lived on, and that in their actions they were hardly free agents, being always driven forward by the fear of the ruffians over whom they were supposed to rule.

In A.D. 1770 it is related that a Turk, who was probably drunk, struck the English consul-general, and when brought before the Dey remained unrepentant, asserting that the infidel should always be smitten by any true believer. The Dey no doubt agreed with him in his heart, but he was not at that time prepared to quarrel with England, and he therefore ordered him to be bastinadoed.

He was bastinadoed until his feet fell off. He then received a thousand blows on his back, and was left to die of hunger and thirst.

An Englishman called William Okely, once a slave in Algiers, thus describes the bastinado. He says, 'They have a strong staff about six feet long, in the middle of which two holes are bored, into which a cord is put, and the ends of the cord fastened on one side the staff with knots so that it makes a loop on the other side. Into this loop both the feet of the person condemned to this punishment are put, then two lusty fellows, one at each end of the staff, lift it up in their arms and twist it about until the feet are fast pinched by the ankles. They raise his feet with the soles upwards as high as their shoulders, the poor man in the meantime resting only with his neck and shoulders on the ground. Then comes another lusty, sturdy knave behind him, and with a tough short truncheon gives him as many violent blows on the soles of his feet as the council may order.'

Two other instances of Algerian ideas of legal punishments will suffice.

Another wretch was sentenced to have his legs and arms broken in three places on an anvil with a hammer. At the twelfth blow life was not extinct. Yet another was crucified (in A.D. 1625) against a wall with four large nails through his hands and feet, whilst a red-hot iron was thrust through both cheeks to prevent his speaking, and then he was slowly burnt to death with firebrands. However, this is enough of such horrors. We will now consider the actual state of the Deys who ruled over Algiers.

In A.D. 1815 Hadj Ali was the Dey. The story runs that seventy Turks wished to put him to death and to elevate the Aga Omar in his place, as he was popular with the soldiery. On warning the said Omar, however, he strongly dissuaded them from their attempt, not because he loved the Dey, but because he had no wish to become the occupier of the dangerous vacated seat. However, when the conspirators agreed to pass him by and to proclaim an official named Mohammed Dey, he had no objections to helping them, and so as to avoid any scandal, they arranged with the various functionaries of state, and quietly did the Dey to death and appointed Mohammed as his successor without any public outcry, as the wretched Hadj Ali was considered rather a coward, and his subjects did not regret him. However, they were not much better pleased with his successor Mohammed, and after he had reigned seventeen days, they strangled him in prison by order of the council. Omar was now persuaded to take the dangerous place. Being a strong, determined man, he proceeded to introduce a severe discipline into the army and the militia, at the same time improving their pay. However, the armed mob, who called themselves the soldiers or militia of Algiers, preferred their liberty, and asserted their rights by strangling Omar on September 8, 1817.

The next Dey was named Ali Khodja. He, being undesirous of meeting the same end as his three predecessors, decided to transfer his residence from the palace to the citadel, which was known as the Kasbah. This place was surrounded by good walls and looked down upon the town, and was therefore more suitable for defence than the open palace. As, however, his loyal subjects might not care for their lord and master putting himself out of their immediate reach in this manner, the move had to be carried out at night, and by stealth. The way this was executed savoured of the tales of the time of the Arabian Nights.

Ten days after his election the Dey issued an order that no Turk under pain of death should be outside his barracks after six o'clock at night. Before the militia had recovered from their surprise, he had the whole of his treasure, estimated at twelve million pounds sterling, his family and his personal guard transferred to the citadel. He wisely formed a large and faithful guard of black slaves and Moors, and, supported by various sections of the people, he was able to hold his own against the dominant party of Turks, and even to carry the war into their country, by causing some 1,800 of the Janizaries or Turkish Regulars to be put to death in a few months. Ali Khodja had a chief minister named Hussein, who had been at a military college in Constantinople, and having entered the Turkish

Artillery as an officer, had found it necessary to hurriedly quit Turkey on account of some small military offence. He fled to Algiers, then a refuge for all vagabonds of Turkish origin who possessed courage and ability to fight, for the Regular Army was entirely recruited from such adventurers; but when one arrived who was already a soldier, and was also able to read and to write, he was indeed a treasure, and his advancement was very rapid. In A.D. 1818 the plague carried off Ali Khodja, and Hussein was elected unanimously as his successor.

Hussein was a very able man, and from this time on, everything began to improve. Security and order, of a sort, became the rule in the town; whilst in the neighbouring country the taxes were peaceably paid. It will be seen from the foregoing narratives that neither the subjects nor the rulers in Algeria had any assured safety for life or property. Justice practically did not exist, whilst the very ruler was quietly 'removed' with all legal ceremony by his own council until he fled to a castle, and guarded his life like a robber chief by gathering one band of brigands to coerce the others.

Now, however, we must discuss the events which led up to the French invasion, and the reasons for this course from the French side.

When the Turks arrived at Algiers in the sixteenth century, they found that the French already had trading establishments ashore at Boné, &c. At these places they bought grain, hides, &c., from the natives, and also carried on a coral fishery. This was continued up to about A.D. 1792, the French paying a rent to the Dey. After that date the Dey, who had quarrelled with the French Government, handed over the fishery to the English, still at a yearly rent. In A.D. 1816, however, he withdrew these rights from the English and again handed them over to the French for some £10,000 a year. He stated to the French consul in A.D. 1827 that he had heard that the Christians had landed fortress guns at their station at Calle, and that he would not allow any Christians to have fortified places on Algerian soil. Probably, however, the whole of the above statement was trumped up by the Dey to give him an excuse to quarrel with France, for besides the supposed arming of a fort at Calle, there was a further point which rankled in his mind, and this was as follows.

When Napoleon took Malta on his way to Egypt, he made a contract for victualling Malta and his own army with two Jews of Algiers, named Bacri. As, however, the Dey of that time became embroiled with France, the contract was not entirely fulfilled, as the Dey prevented it being carried out; yet a large sum of money, amounting to £280,000, was owing to the Jewish brothers Bacri. About A.D. 1819 the French Government proposed to pay off this debt, and in intimating that it would be paid they announced that a sufficient sum would be retained from the total amount to pay the French creditors. In other words, the French creditors of the Bacri were to receive preferential treatment, and their debts were to be paid, so soon as they had proved that they were owing, in a French court of justice. Hussein the Dey appears to have thought this unfair, and the two grievances combined brought on a quarrel between him and the French consul. He was reported to have struck the French consul, though he appears only to have touched him with a fan; but it was eagerly seized upon, and resulted in an ultimatum from the French Government that if an ample apology was not made, and the French flag hoisted on shore and saluted with one hundred guns, a blockade would be established. As the Dey declined to make any apology, the blockade was duly established in June 1827.

It is only fair to add, that the French Government was most anxious to push on a war with a weak foreign Power, as it was hoped that such a war, if crowned with victory, as it practically must be, would direct people's thoughts from criticising the Government at home to discussing the glorious doings of their armies abroad, and also from the Dey's side that, if he had acceded to the French demands, his interesting and turbulent subjects would probably have risen in revolt, and he would have been obliged to bombard his own town into submission, from his citadel, if his garrison had remained faithful.

CHAPTER II

THE French blockading squadron consisted of five frigates, one corvette, and six smaller men-of-war, whilst a further fleet watched the Western Mediterranean, and special men-of-war escorted the French merchant shipping as far as Cadiz. Nevertheless, two French merchantmen were taken and pillaged by their disreputable enemies. Sir Lambert Playfair states that the blockade was of such a feeble nature that its inefficiency excited the ridicule of the Turks in Algiers against whom it was directed. The fleet from Algiers even tried to break out in October 1827, but after a couple of hours' fighting decided to return to the shelter of the harbour. Two other trifling successes came to the French in the following year (A.D. 1828), when they cut out and carried off a captured French ship under the guns of Mers-el-Kebir; and again, when they destroyed some four piratical craft, also under the guns of a fort. Against these, however, had to be placed a small disaster whereby three French men-of-war's boats were wrecked, and of twenty-five officers and men who had landed from the wrecks, twenty-four were killed and one was taken prisoner.

A final attempt was made in July 1829 to arrange matters peaceably, and a French man-of-war under a flag of truce arrived in Algiers Harbour, and its commander had two hours' conversation with the Dey.

But it was too late. The populace of Algiers, having existed for 300 years as pirates, were of opinion that nothing could really interfere with their trade, and they howled at the French officers all the way to the kasbah, and finally manned the guns and opened fire on the French ship as she sailed slowly out of the harbour, still flying the flag of truce. Hussein, the Dey, punished some of the ringleaders of this breach of public faith, but he probably was secretly pleased to find that his people were heart and soul with him in a determination to resist any Christian Power's demand to the utmost extremity.

Nothing was now left to France but to settle these differences by the sword, and to deal so sharply with these barbarians that they would gladly sue for peace. But now a curious thing happened. The Pasha or Khedive of Egypt, Mehemet Ali, made the startling offer to conquer Algeria with his own troops if the French Government would give him a loan of nearly £1,000,000, repayable in ten years, and would also give him four ships of the line.

This curious offer was actually entertained by the French Government, but the Sultan refused to allow his vassal Mehemet Ali to undertake the expedition. The French Government finally gave as its reason for declining Mehemet Ali's offer with reference to the ships, that any ship of the line on which the French flag had floated could not be handed over to a foreign Power and sail under its flag, consistently with the French national honour. England was very suspicious at the time of France's intentions, and as she considered that the trade of Algeria, as a whole, was some seven millions sterling per annum, she would

THE CONQUEST OF ALGERIA

rather have seen the Pasha of Egypt as the owner by conquest of this territory than the French, as England rather selfishly put the idea of trade before the question as to the necessity of destroying such a set of pirates as the Turks in Algiers. Probably the Egyptians would not have been able to carry out the conquest, even if it had been given into their hands by consent of England, France, and Turkey.

In February 1830, Vice-Admiral Duperré was directed to take charge of the naval part of the expedition, which was to be equipped at Toulon. April was decided upon as the best month for the expedition, but the French Admiralty demanded eight months for preparations, which would bring the date of sailing into September. After some debate they consented to be ready by July, but the Government allowed them only till May. The fleet consisted of eleven ships of the line, twenty-four frigates, and sixty-five corvettes and brigs, whilst three hundred and forty-seven merchantmen formed the convoy; not to mention one hundred and fifty small sailing boats, such as feluccas, which were added for the purpose of disembarkation. The troops and the war material were embarked on the men-of-war, whilst the merchant vessels transported the horses and forage for them, and rations for the men. These three hundred and forty-seven vessels were principally loaded at Marsailles.

And now to speak of the *military* part of the expeditionary force. 29,224 infantry were detailed for the enterprise. This infantry was formed into three divisions, each division was made up of three brigades, whilst each brigade again consisted of two regiments of two battalions each. A lieutenant-general was appointed to command each division, and it is a curious commentary on the divided state of France to find that one general had to be chosen from the generals of Napoleon's empire, another from the Restoration party of 1815, whilst yet a third was a Royalist of the old school. They were named respectively Baron Berthezéme, Count de Loverdo, and the Duc des Cars.

To a soldier, it is worthy of notice that the regiments were 'composite' ones; that is to say, they were made up from different corps, but to a great extent the battalions were kept intact, though they were carefully culled of all weakly men, and the battalion then had brought into it sufficient men to make it up to war strength from the other battalions, of the same regiment, and when this was insufficient, then reserve men of the district where the regiment was stationed were called up to complete the battalion, even though they might not belong to that regiment.

The cavalry, about five hundred strong, also was a 'composite' regiment, or, as the Great Napoleon used to call it, a 'Regiment de marche.' One-third of the regiment were armed with lances. The Field Artillery consisted of four batteries, and there further was a mountain battery, but the calibre of the guns is not mentioned, whilst, knowing that a siege must form part of the operations, a siege park was included, consisting of thtiry 24-pounders with 1,000 rounds apiece, twenty 16-pounders and twelve 12-pounders with 800 rounds apiece, twelve 8-inch howitzers and eight 10-inch mortars, all these last with only 500 rounds each. Ten companies of what we should now

THE CONQUEST OF ALGERIA

call Garrison Artillery were told off to the siege guns.

Added to this, there were also taken 500 congreve war rockets, and the artillery had further at their disposal a company of the pontoon train and a company of artificers.

They also provided for siege purposes 100,000 sand-bags, and 5,000,000 cartridges as a reserve for the infantry, besides more than 250 tons of powder. A balloon was also taken, but was never used during the short campaign.

The engineers comprised some 1,350 officers and men, amongst them being six companies of sappers and two of miners. A very large supply of working tools was also provided.

The rationing of the troops was carried on through a contractor, the average number of men's rations calculated on being 40,000 daily, with 4,000 horse or mule rations; and two months' provisions at this rate were embarked in the convoy.

Arrangements were also made for hospital accommodation, and by the courtesy of the Spanish Government a sort of base hospital was opened at Port Mahon, capable of containing 2,000 sick and wounded, whilst the advanced or field hospitals were intended to hold at least 150 beds.

Some 5,000 tents were taken for the troops, but the train only consisted of 128 2-wheeled carts and the same number of 4-wheeled wagons, with some 630 pack mules. Truly a marvellously small transport corps for so large a force!

A very interesting feature was that twenty-five interpreters were selected from the old Mamalukes of the Imperial Guard, and were found to be most useful. Some blockhouses were even constructed in France ready to be transported complete to Algeria. With true foresight, a reserve corps was also organised of all branches of the service. It numbered some 8,500 of all ranks.

Not unnaturally, the command of this expedition was much sought after. Marshal Marmont and M. de Bourmont were the two most probable personages to be selected, and the latter was finally chosen in April. He was at the time Minister of War in the French Government, and is probably best known previous to this as being the general who deserted from Napoleon to the Allies on the 15th June 1815. Why he did so need not be here discussed, but he not unnaturally wished to have his name associated with some other and more honourable event in his military career. Hence his anxiety to take this command.

It would, however, be worth while to consider for a moment what the Dey of Algiers could oppose to this formidable invasion.

Algeria, as has already been said, was divided into four commands or 'Beyliks'; 15,000 Turks were, roughly, the garrison and the governing race. The 'governed' amounted to some 3,000,000 souls, of whom the greater part consisted of most warlike races, strengthened by the 'Coulouglis' or half-bred Turks. These 15,000 men ruled the country by setting one tribe against another. Thus, a strong Arab tribe would be selected and sent to collect taxes from some of the weaker ones. The stronger tribe would be freed from taxes themselves on condition of enforcing the payment on the others, and, further, a certain

THE CONQUEST OF ALGERIA 25

percentage of the taxes so collected would be given to them. If the weaker tribes objected to paying their taxes, the stronger tribe would be backed up by the heavy arm of the Turk. Thus the native inhabitants were played off one against the other, and the Turk remained more or less master throughout. The Kabyles in their mountains, however, were rather an exception, for there they bid defiance to Turk and Arab, and though several attempts had been made to conquer their fastnesses, the results had always been disastrous to the invader.

So well known was the fact that the Kabyles could defend their mountains against Arabs and Turks, that a proverb was current in Algiers to the effect that the rule of the Turk extended so far as he could ride his horse. Where the horse could not go (viz. into the mountains), there the rule of the Turk ended.

It would appear then, despite the fact that practically all the male inhabitants of the country were warriors, that there was so much internal strife and unrest, that but little united resistance was to be expected. This, however, curiously enough, was a wrong assumption, for all the inhabitants, being Mahomedans, were always ready to leave off their internal feuds for the moment to fight with the Christian. So really the forces at the disposal of the Dey were most numerous and warlike, though highly irregular, and the number of his force was only limited by the number of the inhabitants of the country, and by the number he chose to collect, of that population, for any engagement. His arms were also quite good, though most of his muskets were flint locks—that was quite usual for all armies at the time. Strangely enough, the fortifications of Algiers were practically all made to look seaward. The land defences were quite poor, so that the town was much more liable to be taken easily by an attack from the land side by a small army, than it would be to succumb to a bombardment by a powerful fleet from the sea.

CHAPTER III

THE army commenced to embark on the 11th of May 1830, and despite bad weather it was all on board by the 17th; but detained by a calm, the fleet was not able to proceed until the 25th of May, on which date they finally set sail. The rendezvous was at the Balearic Isles. The convoy, however, did not sail well, and some days were spent collecting it together. On the 29th of May they again left their anchorage, and had already arrived within sight of the Algerian coast when a heavy storm arose, and the French were driven back in the direction from which they had come. The admiral issued directions to reunite in the Bay of Palma. By the 9th of June the whole fleet and convoy were together again and refitted, on the 10th the anchorage was left, and on the 13th of June, as day broke, Algiers appeared as a fairy city through the fog. It had been decided to land at a small bay some twelve miles, as the crow flies, to the west of Algiers, so the fleet stood steadily towards this place, which now needs to be described.

A point of land ran out some 1,100 yards into the sea, with a bay on either side. The tongue of land was some 550 yards broad, and ended seawards in a mass of rock, but towards the land was sandy and low, and ran out in a succession of dunes to a plain of rather more fertile soil, with low brushwood, &c., scattered about.

The name of this place was Sidi Ferruch, which it took from a Mahomedan saint's tomb placed on the end of the cape. To the surprise of all, a small Turkish fort on the western side of the promontory was found to be dismantled, which was very satisfactory for the invaders, as it would probably have rendered the disembarkation more difficult as its guns commanded the western sands of the cape. Of course, it could not have maintained a fight with the men-of-war, but it was questionable if men-of-war could lie in close enough to do it great damage on account of the depth of water. The eastern side of this convenient cape was not used by the fleet, excepting on one occasion, as the bay was small and cramped. As the fleet drew in towards the land they saw mounted men, both Turks and Arabs, brandishing their weapons and gesticulating as they galloped about the sandy beach, the whole forming a most picturesque scene.

By the evening of the 13th of June the whole armada was duly anchored (excepting the horse transports) in the selected places, and everything was ready for the disembarkation, which was arranged for the next day. The Turks were found to have withdrawn from the spit of land itself; but they had concentrated their forces to attack any troops issuing from the promontory, and had placed cannon in batteries to assist them. These cannon did open fire on the fleet, but the distance was too great, and few rounds were fired and no damage was done.

But whilst the French fleet had been slowly struggling across from France to the Bay of Sidi Ferruch, the French Navy had suffered a small disaster as follows. Two men-of-war had been wrecked, small brigs, with a crew of about 100 seamen each. One man only was lost, but the 200 men found themselves on the Algerian coast some fifty miles east of Algiers, with arms certainly, but with their powder spoilt by the water. Attacked by the Kabyles and every other tribe in the neighbourhood, they surrendered as prisoners of war; but another French brig, arriving some few days later to make inquiries about the wrecks and the fate of the prisoners, was fired upon and returned the fire, and in revenge most of the unfortunate prisoners were massacred by the natives. When the few who had escaped the slaughter were marched into Algiers, they passed under the heads of 110 of their comrades who had been done to death, and whose heads were exposed as trophies on the gates of Algiers. The Dey had also well employed his time by enrolling all the citizens of Algiers to help defend the fortifications, and by sending for all the neighbouring tribes of Kabyles and Arabs to come and assist him to defeat the French invasion, whilst the Beys of Constantine and Oran sent 13,000 troops each to his camp, and the Bey of Titteri brought his force, somewhat smaller in numbers, to swell the Turkish array. The whole army was under command of the son-in-law of the Dey, who was named Ibrahim. They were camped near the mouth of the Harrach, where a landing would have been feasible, which place was south-east of Algiers; but a strong detachment watched the anchorage of Sidi Ferruch, as has been said.

Politics do not enter very largely into our present history, but they to a great extent affect all campaigns, and this one was no exception to the rule. As has been already mentioned, England was very much exercised at the step that France was taking, and many interviews took place between the French ambassador in London and Lord Aberdeen, Minister for Foreign Affairs in the English Government, with reference to the expedition. Further discussions ensued in the French Cabinet as to what was to be done with Algiers and Algeria when they had been conquered. The Sultan of Turkey sent an ambassador to Algiers in the person of an admiral. He was refused permission to pass through the French blockading squadron, and, escorted by a French frigate, sailed for France. Meeting the French armada *en route*, he was most anxious that they should return with him to France, but the French admiral and M. de Bourmont, not unnaturally, did not see their way to oblige him. The two adjoining states of Tripoli and Tunis had decided on the course they proposed to pursue. Tunis was frankly neutral, whilst Tripoli was anxious to support Algiers in the struggle against the infidel, but unfortunately for Algiers, Mehemet Ali was threatening to invade Tripoli, and the ruler of this state decided to keep his army at home to protect his own dominions, whilst he recommended the Dey to the care of Mahomet. The correspondence between the Dey of Algiers and the Bey of Tripoli was found in the citadel at Algiers after the capture of that town by the French. It was of a most interesting description, contained many curses against the French, and many prayers for the success of the arms of the faithful, and wound up by hinting that the Dey's cause was so good that Providence

THE CONQUEST OF ALGERIA 31

would see that he came to no harm, despite the fact that the army of Tripoli was too busy to move to his assistance.

To return to the French force in the bay at Sidi Ferruch. At two o'clock on the morning of the 14th of June, the troops were paraded for the attempt to land; each man, besides all his arms and accoutrements, carried five days' provisions. Six battalions, two field batteries, and one company of engineers could be landed at the same time, and three battalions were taken from each of the first two brigades of the 1st Division. The fleet had brought from France, on the decks of the ships of the line and of the frigates, large flat boats for this disembarkation. These boats would carry either 150 infantry or a couple of field guns without horses. Each flat boat was towed by a man-of-war's boat with twelve rowers. At 4 a.m. a signal was given, and each boat rowed vigorously for the shore, towing its flat boat if it was attached to one. At first regular line was maintained, but as the boats neared the shore, each strove to be first to land, and the soldiers in the flat boats each cheered their man-of-war's boat crew, and urged them on. The landing was effected without difficulty, and the boats returned for a further human cargo.

At five o'clock the 1st Division, still incomplete, moved off towards the Turkish position already mentioned, and some Arab skirmishers in the bushes at once opened a scattered fire of musketry, but almost immediately afterwards disappeared, whilst the Turkish cannon opened a fire upon the French at 1,400 yards' range. To answer this the French field guns replied, being drawn along with their advancing troops by the gunners, as no horses had been landed. At the same time three small men-of-war opened a fire from the eastern side of the cape, and drew off the enemy's fire from the troops. The French in the meantime halted, their general having received orders not to attack until his last two battalions had landed. Whilst halted, they took covert in the folds of the ground and awaited support. About six o'clock M. de Bourmont arrived, trudging on foot over the sand, and at seven o'clock, the remaining two battalions belonging to the 1st Division having arrived, the whole moved steadily forward to attack the Turkish batteries. As they commenced to move they were charged by 500 mounted Arabs. The charge consisted of each yelling individual galloping down, choosing his own time, and as soon as he had approached near enough to suit his fancy, he raised his long gun and fired at the French, and then wheeled sharply away and galloped off, reloading as he galloped, and continued this curious attack. Colonel Scott, apparently an English soldier of fortune, who served in the 18th Spanish Infantry, and afterwards with the celebrated Abd-el-Kader for a short time, has left in his diary the following account of the method of fighting adopted by the native horsemen in Algiers. He says—

'They set their horse to full speed, laying themselves down on his neck so that only his head is to be seen. When they arrive at point-blank distance they rise up in their stirrups and fire their piece, and wheeling to the left-about they are out of sight like lightning in the same manner as they came, being protected from

THE CONQUEST OF ALGERIA 33

receiving any dishonourable wound from the immense back which Arab saddles have.'

To young troops armed only with inaccurate muskets, such a method of attack must have been very disconcerting, though it is probable that the fire of the Arabs would be still more inaccurate than that of the French infantry.

The French skirmishers, however, easily defeated this irregular cavalry, and after killing some, drove the remainder away. A thousand yards from the battery the 1st Brigade moved round the enemy's left, whilst the 2nd Brigade attacked their front. The Turkish fire, badly directed, principally went over the heads of the French, though some few shots took effect. The enemy's gunners, however, wisely fled as the French troops came to close quarters, leaving twelve cannon and two bronze mortars, with ammunition, to the victors. Thirty-two killed and wounded was the total French loss. Any who fell into the hands of the Arabs were at once beheaded and otherwise mutilated. By one o'clock all the infantry were landed, and whilst the 1st and 2nd Divisions bivouacked in front of the captured position, the 3rd Division remained as a garrison for the cape, and the engineers constructed a work from bay to bay on the landward end of the promontory of Sidi Ferruch, whilst the sailors sent ashore as fast as possible the stores of all descriptions. A stroke of good luck was the finding of water for drinking purposes on the promontory after sinking wells for some 17 feet. As night fell, the Arab skirmishers crept up and opened fire on the two leading divisions.

About 2 a.m. on the 15th of June a loose horse

startled a sentry, who at once fired into the darkness and gave the alarm. The men nearest him instantly seized their arms, and commenced to fire wildly into the night, and for a quarter of an hour the two divisions continued to fire at nothing. Then the drums sounded the 'Cease Fire!' and the men at last obeyed the signal and the firing ceased. Sixteen killed and wounded was the result of this panic, all injured by the French, as the enemy had taken no part in the affair. At daybreak the skirmishing was renewed by the Arabs, but a few shells from the mountain battery drove them away.

The 15th and 16th of June were occupied in landing still more stores. The morning of the 16th was made very unpleasant by a dreadful storm. Such a sea got up in a short time that some of the convoy, with seven feet of water under their keels, were knocking themselves to pieces on the bottom, owing, of course, to sinking in the trough of the waves. Fortunately by noon the storm was past.

On the 17th, proclamations were distributed to the Arabs, pointing out that the French quarrel was only with the Dey of Algiers. These proclamations were distributed by the hands of an old Arab, who had come to the French under a flag of truce, probably really as a spy, and by one of the interpreters, who had his head cut off by the Dey for his trouble. Sir Lambert Playfair mentions that in Algiers at the present day, the stone on which this unfortunate man had his head '*sawn*' off, is still preserved. It is a Moorish fountain with twisted columns, and stands in the Officers' Club in the city of Algiers.

THE CONQUEST OF ALGERIA 35

The brave man, whose name was George Garoué, volunteered for this dangerous service; and when the almost absolute certainty of detection and death was pointed out to him, only replied that he had enjoyed the hospitality of France for some thirty years, and it would be a shameful thing if he could make her any return and was deterred by the fear of death. (He was not French by descent.)

On the 18th of June the Turkish forces were increased by the arrival of Ibrahim from the mouth of the Harrach with troops, consisting of 5,000 Janizaries, or regular Turkish infantry; 5,000 Coulouglis, or half-bred Turks, who were also infantry; 10,000 Moors from Algiers; 30,000 Arabs, and 10,000 Kabyles. Altogether some 60,000 armed men were drawn up to oppose the French advance.

At daybreak on the 19th of June the Arabs, favoured by the fog, commenced a heavy skirmish with the outposts, and at once two strong columns were seen to be approaching under cover of this fire to turn the French flanks. The enemy's left column consisted of 1,000 Janizaries, 6,000 Kabyles, and 20,000 Arabs, and was commanded by the Bey of Constantine.

This column was repulsed by the repeated discharges of the mountain battery of six howitzers, aided by a charge by the 15th Regiment of the Line. The enemy's right column, which consisted of practically the remainder of his 60,000 men, was led forward by the Aga Ibrahim in person. His design was to break through between the French left and the sea, as there was a large gap on the left flank, unoccupied by any troops. Fortunately for the

French, five companies had that morning been sent in to fill up this gap. The Turkish column pushed them backwards, and they retired fighting in the fog, whilst a brigade of the 2nd Division, which had been held in reserve, was hurriedly sent up at the double to their support.

After a sharp hand-to-hand struggle the Turks fled in disorder, pursued by the French infantry and shelled by the French brigs, which were guarding the eastern bay. The enemy's cavalry boldly attacked the French centre, bravely leaping their horses over or into the entrenchments, and struggling hand to hand with the French infantry. Some of the entrenchments were lost, particularly those held by the 37th Regiment, whilst the 14th Regiment were able to hold their ground. The French, however, on the defeat of the two Turkish columns attacked in their turn with the bayonet and cleared the enemy out of their entrenchments after a hard struggle. The whole French line now advanced, driving Kabyle and Arab skirmishers before it, the field batteries being drawn by hand. Up to now the fighting had been carried on by the first two divisions, and under the orders of their lieutenant-generals. Now, however, the commander-in-chief, Count de Bourmont, rode up, bringing with him two brigades of the 3rd Division as a reserve. The Aga Ibrahim had rallied his troops, and the whole now formed a strong line in front of their camp. It being only seven o'clock, the generals held a consultation as to what was to be done. During this consultation the Turkish fire became heavier. The French were ordered to attack at once, and to attempt to gain the enemy's left flank, for the purpose of

THE CONQUEST OF ALGERIA 37

crushing it, and driving the whole army from their line of retreat to Algiers, and if possible to press them towards the sea, where they could be brought under the fire of the French ships, and perhaps be compelled to surrender in large masses. Unfortunately, the French right was delayed by the bad ground, and the Turks were attacked at all points at the same time. Many of the gunners refused to leave their pieces and were killed on them. The French still steadily advanced with their cannon, showering round shot on the masses of the enemy, and into their camp, in front of which they were fighting, whilst congreve rockets carried terror into the hearts of the Arab cavaliers, who were unacquainted with these weapons. By noon the French were drawn up in line beyond the Turkish camp, and large clouds of dust told where the enemy were flying towards Algiers and towards the distant hills. The French losses were 57 killed and 473 wounded. The enemy's was not known, as their habit of carrying off their dead and wounded prevented accurate estimates from being made; but large numbers of wounded and dead were left by them this day, proving how hurried their flight was. Large supplies were found in the captured camp by the French; and after a month of salt provisions, fresh meat was greatly appreciated by all ranks.

CHAPTER IV

On the 22nd of June the horse transports began to arrive from Palma. They had great difficulty in weathering the point of Sidi Ferruch owing to currents and a light wind, and the French general on the 23rd sent out a party towards the sea coast to see if he could not possibly land the horses nearer Algiers, but no safe place could be found. Whilst this party was out, the Arabs again commenced skirmishing with the French outposts, and it soon became evident that the enemy had plucked up courage, and had determined to strike another blow at the infidels. The reason was not far to seek : the ulemas, or holy men of the Mahomedan faith, were inciting all Musselmen to join in the attack, promising them an easy victory; and, further, the immobility of the French made the natives think that they must have suffered very severely in the last attack. Under these circumstances some 20,000 Kabyles and Arabs returned to the Aga, whilst, of course, he had his Turkish troops still under him. The Dey wisely anticipated Abraham Lincoln's sage advice, 'Never swap horses when crossing a stream,' and left his son-in-law, Ibrahim, in charge, sending him kindly messages of regret for his ill-success of the 19th June, and urging him to destroy the invaders in the next battle.

During the morning of the 24th of June the Turks

THE CONQUEST OF ALGERIA 39

massed their troops in front of the French outposts. The French at once moved four brigades out to the attack, each regiment in double column, with skirmishers thrown out in front, and the artillery marched in the intervals in line with the skirmishers. The fire of the artillery alone drove the enemy away in the wildest disorder. Despite the roughness of the ground, broken by ravines and clumps of aloes, &c., the French maintained a good line. At two o'clock a powder magazine of the enemy's blew up, causing as much consternation in the French Army as in the Turkish forces, as the French rank and file were somehow convinced that it simply meant that the ground was mined, and that this was one of the mines exploding. Finally the army was halted, after driving the enemy back some six miles. The French right rested on the Dely Hrahim, a square building used as a sort of farm. The Arabs made an effort to retake this place, and in the struggle one of the sons of General de Bourmont was mortally wounded. Four of the general's sons were in the field at the time as officers of the French Army. It was noticed after the battle, that the Arabs had had the audacity to move in between the camp and the four French brigades, and had killed any stragglers they had been able to lay hands upon, and had even threatened to attack the camp.

The French now moved up the 3rd Division from Sidi Ferruch, sending back one of the brigades of the 2nd Division to act as garrison of the cape, which was now thoroughly fortified and was one huge depôt of stores. As the 3rd Division moved up the Arabs threw themselves on their baggage, for which they had omitted to detail an escort, and plundered it.

Several of the French soldiers died of sunstroke on this march.

The Dey now determined to try changing his general, and he placed the Bey of Titteri in command. He at once ordered the irregulars to attack the flanks and stragglers on all occasions, whilst he put his regulars and his picked marksmen in front of the French, and subjected the latter to a severe musketry fire. He further placed cannon to take the French lines in enfilade. Between the 25th and 28th of June the 3rd Division alone had 520 men killed and wounded as a result of this change of tactics of the enemy. Early on the 28th of June everything looked very threatening. Some 2,000 Arab cavalry were massed in front of the French to support the Arab marksmen, who maintained a steady and deadly fire.

About nine o'clock in the morning this fire died away, and the commander of the 4th Light Infantry, which had sustained a large part of this fighting, gave the order to clean the muskets. No sooner had the men commenced to carry out the order than the Kabyles rushed from ravines and other hiding-places upon them, whilst the Arab cavalry galloped in, and commenced to use their sabres in deadly earnest. It would have fared ill with this regiment, if two battalions, one from the 2nd and the other from the 3rd Line Regiment, had not attacked the Kabyles from either side and driven them off. The enemy returned a second time to the attack, but were again driven off. The 4th Light Infantry alone lost eight officers and 117 men in killed and wounded.

The French commander-in-chief noted that the enemy gained confidence from day to day, and determined to bring this waiting game to a finish so soon as possible. All his horses were now landed, and the siege guns had been dragged up by the evening of the 28th of June to his army, so he determined at once to move forward to attack the defences of the city of Algiers. The chief bulwark was known as the Château de l'Empereur. It was a sort of stone castle on the top of a height which dominated the town, and here the Emperor Charles the Fifth of Spain had pitched his tent, during the ill-fated expedition which he led against that city. This point was afterwards fortified by the Turks, who perceived its great importance. To the French soldiers, however, there was only one emperor, and they connected it in some mysterious way with Napoleon the Great.

M. de Bourmont then drew all his troops from the depôt at Sidi Ferruch, excepting one battalion, as the fleet had landed 1,400 men to assist in maintaining it against any sudden attack, and he issued orders to his troops to move at three o'clock on the morning of the 29th June. He determined that, as his army was too small to invest the whole of Algiers, he would simply attack the main defences of the town. The advance was made in three columns, with the 1st Division on the right, the 2nd in the centre, and the 3rd on the left. The 1st Division marched upon the Château de l'Empereur on the right, whilst the left column marched first upon Bouzaria, and then on towards the crest of the hills, immediately behind and overlooking Algiers. One brigade from each division was left to cover the communications, as these were daily threatened, and the convoys attacked, by the Arabs and Kabyles.

The Turks were more or less surprised by the French advance, and after some fighting fled. By six o'clock the 3rd Division had established themselves within cannon shot of the kasbah, or citadel, of Algiers. Here they found all the unfortunate Jews of Algiers —men, women, and children—who had been turned out of the city by the Dey. The French soldiers killed many of the men before they realised that these poor creatures were not enemies. Then the remainder were sent for protection to Sidi Ferruch.

With reference to the constant ill-treatment accorded to the Jews by the inhabitants of Northern Africa, the Colonel Scott before mentioned notes in his diary that he found the reason practically lay in a tradition amongst some of the tribes of that coast, that their forefathers were Canaanites driven out of Palestine by the Israelites under Joshua, and they thus felt it was almost a duty to treat them badly. He gives a case of two wretched Jews who had been made prisoners for assisting the French. They were sold by public auction. The Arabs bid up to £48 for the two, simply to have the pleasure, after the purchase, of cutting their heads off; but the miserable men were saved by the other Jews clubbing together, and bidding 4s. more for them.

An amusing error caused great delay to the French. It being a foggy morning, as they looked down on the plain running away south from Algiers they saw only mist, which was mistaken for the sea. After examining their maps they decided that the maps were wrong, and that Algiers was north-east of Bouzaria, where the 3rd Division stood, and the 2nd

THE CONQUEST OF ALGERIA

and 1st Divisions, which were now in their right places, were ordered to move directly to their left. Despite the objections of their respective commanders, who could see that they were in their right places, the divisions had to comply, and the confusion became very great as they moved along the crests of the mountains or in the ravines, according as each commander thought the one or the other appeared the most practicable. As the mist cleared away the general saw his error, but the troops were so mixed up by this time that he found it more easy to send the 3rd Division to the right, whilst the 2nd Division remained in the centre, and the 1st Division took the left. This crossing of troops was very confusing: many men lost their regiments, and many fell by the wayside from the effects of the heat. Fortunately the enemy did not attack.

Since that day the mists have been greatly reduced around the city of Algiers by the draining of large marshes, from which the mists arose. Incidentally the health of the city and surrounding country has improved. Malarial fever has become more rare, and the mosquitoes, which used to render life a burden to all Europeans, have almost vanished away.

It is necessary to describe the Château de l'Empereur. Constructed in the sixteenth century, it was a good example of Turkish fortifications of that time. It was of rectangular shape, each face being about 175 yards in length. The walls were of cut stone, some 45 feet high, and 13 feet thick. Each corner was flanked by a small bastion. The Dey, since the quarrel with France had broken out, had constructed a second wall on the south-eastern face of the château. In the middle of the fortress was a very thick, squat, round tower, which formed a sort of keep. The enemy used this as their powder magazine. The walls were not defended by a ditch, though it was known that a ditch had been begun around the château. Still, it was so little advanced that it was, for all practical purposes, non-existent.

It can, then, be clearly seen how important a position was occupied by this sort of fort, when one considers that it commanded the citadel, the town of Algiers, the harbour, and all the roads leading out of the town to the south-east. The château was some 675 feet above the sea level.

Some 850 yards to the north-east was the citadel, which was 120 feet lower than the château. The citadel formed the apex of the triangle, which was the shape of the town of Algiers, and from it ran, on either side, an old wall between 35 and 40 feet high; at its foot was a triangular ditch about 25 feet deep, whilst on the outer side of the ditch was a loopholed wall about 6 feet high. The sea front, which formed the base of the triangle, was defended by a wall and then by many powerful forts. As almost all the attacks so far had come from the sea, the Deys had contented themselves with strengthening their sea front, whilst their town was almost defenceless to an attack from land.

Algiers is built on the site of the ancient town of Icosium. Pliny mentions that the Emperor Vespasian created it a 'Latin' city, which meant in those days a city of greater importance than an 'Italian' city, but one of less importance than a 'Roman' city. In A.D. 411 mention is made of a Christian bishop of

THE CONQUEST OF ALGERIA

that town, and, finally, in A.D. 914 the Mahomedans founded this town on the ruins of Icosium, and called it 'El Jezair,' which means the 'Islands of the children of Mezghanna' in abbreviated form.

In A.D. 1067 it is mentioned as containing many splendid monuments of antiquity, but these have now vanished away.

CHAPTER V

No opposition was offered on the afternoon of the 29th of June to the French, and the commander-in-chief, accompanied by his artillery and engineer generals, made an inspection of the ground. A battalion of the 49th Regiment with some artillery had wandered (in the confusion mentioned before) under the shelter of a ridge 750 yards from the Château de l'Empereur, and here he decided to open his first parallel. The enemy was so supine that he had not done more than fire a few cannon shots at the 49th Regiment, but the Kabyles and Arabs hung like a threatening cloud on the hills to the south and south-east, viz. on the French right front and right flank.

The first parallel did not, however, make much progress that evening, as the men were worn out with the marching and counter-marching. It should, perhaps, be mentioned that one neglect of the Turks gave the French a great advantage, and that was, that all the neighbouring houses outside the walls had either cisterns or wells attached. The enemy had not taken the trouble to run off the water from the cisterns, nor to fill up, foul, or otherwise destroy the wells. If this had been done, very great inconvenience, if no worse, would have been occasioned to their enemy. As it was, the French were able to refresh themselves at their leisure amongst the houses, gardens, and trees of the villas surrounding the town. How much the French were in need of this rest and refreshment after the extraordinary mixture of the 1st and 3rd Divisions is best shown by the remark, 'That the troops themselves admitted that the day was the most distressing of the whole of the campaign,' and this, it must be remembered, was a day on which there was practically no fighting; whilst M. Rousset states that the two divisions were so mixed in the most inextricable confusion, that *several hours* elapsed before the bulk of some regiments could be got together again.

Next morning, the 30th of June, two battalions were sent out with a couple of mountain howitzers. This force moved, from the French right to the sea on the east side of Algiers, for the purpose of reconnoitring the ground, and of ascertaining whether it was necessary to establish a force on that side, to cut the communications of Algiers with the country south of it, called the Plain of Metidja. It will be remembered that the Arabs and Kabyles had drawn off to the south towards the hills. From there they could easily communicate, by the roads which this column went to reconnoitre, with the garrison of Algiers; and as the French found later at Constantine to their cost, the Kabyle, at least, made an excellent soldier in a besieged town. Thus this reconnaissance was very desirable and was well carried out. It was found, however, that, to permanently establish a force there, would require a larger number of men than the army could spare, so that the project was abandoned.

The same day the Turks by a feigned retreat

drew their adversaries, who pursued them recklessly, under the fire of the Château de l'Empereur, and, amongst others, killed the commandant of the trenches, Major Chamband of the Engineers.

Three batteries were ordered to be made to open fire upon the château, and were named respectively, from the French right, 'Batterie de Bordeaux,' 'Batterie du Roi,' and 'Batterie du Dauphin,' all between 550 and 700 yards from the enemy's work. They were armed as follows: 'Bordeaux,' with two 8-inch howitzers; 'Roi,' with six 24-pounders; and 'Dauphin,' with four 24-pounders, whilst to the left of the 'Dauphin' battery, 100 yards nearer the enemy, four 10-inch mortars were placed. This battery was named 'Batterie Duquesne.' Still further to the French left, and at the same distance from the château, six 16-pounders were placed where they could enfilade the attacked front of the fort, and thus seriously interfere with the enemy's fire. It received the name of 'Batterie de Saint Louis.'

Small skirmishes went on all day during the 30th of June, sometimes developing into severe local combats. For instance, the regiment on the French right, holding a villa which formed the consulate of Sweden, was attacked, and lost fifty-five men killed and wounded. The French replied by raising another battery to bombard the Château de l'Empereur, which they armed with four 8-inch howitzers, and which was about 850 yards from the enemy. It was named 'Batterie Henry IV.'

The French also suffered considerably on their left, as they foolishly neglected to make certain that a ravine leading from the enemy's position was im-

THE CONQUEST OF ALGERIA 49

practicable. Trusting to chance, they established their working parties and were brought to a knowledge of their mistake by a heavy fire directed on these parties by Turkish skirmishers who had somehow managed to scramble up the ravines and the opposite precipices. At first gabions and sand bags were used to cover the working parties, but the enemy was finally driven off by establishing a battery of two field guns to sweep the crests they occupied. Two field guns were also sent to the Swedish consulate. The French also lost another commandant of the trenches, in the person of Major Vaillant of the Engineers, who had succeeded Major Chamband. He was wounded in the leg, and his place had to be taken by Major Lenoir.

To add to the troubles of the besieged, a part of the French fleet stood in on the 1st of July and subjected the sea front to a bombardment during an hour and a half. When one considers that the navy had already landed 1,400 seamen and marines to defend Sidi Ferruch, and that they had just experienced, on the 26th of June, so severe a storm that it had wrecked four of their transports, although anchored in the shelter of the bay, it certainly speaks well for their courage and discipline that they were willing to go in and engage one of the most powerfully defended sea fronts in existence. Little damage was done, but the moral effect must have been immense, both in raising the spirits of the French soldiers, who from the hills were eye-witnesses of the whole combat, and in depressing the spirits of the brave though barbarous enemy, who were thus taken between two fires as it were, and were obliged to divide their forces to man both the threatened fronts of their fortress town. The 1st and 2nd of July passed in small combats, whilst the working parties struggled with the rocky soil. On the 3rd of July the gallant French sailors again brought in some of their ships and engaged the shore batteries for some two hours.

The efforts made by the French fleet become more noticeable when the dispatches of the admiral on the subject are read. He points out that the currents were so violent that two of his ships had already each broken two of their anchors whilst lying on this coast, and that he had been obliged to send two of his precious steamboats to tow them to a place of safety. He urges that if anything happens to the fleet the safety of the army must be compromised, and points out how much more strongly Algiers is now fortified than when Lord Exmouth battered it to pieces with five line of battle ships and some frigates in A.D. 1816. To all this must be added that the admiral and the general belonged to two different political parties, and that party feeling ran very high at that time in France, just before the Revolution of 1830. Nevertheless, despite all these troubles, dangers, and differences of opinion, he nobly sent part of his fleet in, to distract the enemy's attention. It had been hoped that the land batteries would have been able to assist the fleet, but, as almost always happens in sieges, the works were not advanced enough to be armed in the allotted time.

All was ready on the night of the 3rd-4th of July for the bombardment of the Château de l'Empereur, to begin at daybreak on the 4th. The signal was to

THE CONQUEST OF ALGERIA 51

be a rocket fired from the headquarters of the French Army. During the night the Turks made an attack on the 'Dauphin' battery, but the sentinels duly gave the alarm and the attack was repulsed, no damage being done to the battery. As a precaution against attack one infantry company had been detailed to remain in rear of each battery; and to replace any casualties, two companies of garrison artillery remained in readiness at the siege depôt. At 3.45 a.m. the rocket was discharged, and immediately all the guns opened, amidst the cheers of the French Army. The Turks were not expecting the bombardment to commence so soon, but as fast as they were able to man their guns, they replied. Day was just breaking and there was no wind, so in a very short time friend and foe were hidden in a thick cloud of smoke. As the sun rose, however, a breeze sprang up and drove the smoke clouds away, allowing more sure aim to be taken. The masonry of the château soon began to break up under this heavy fire. The shells from the mortars in particular caused grave losses to the enemy, as they apparently had no overhead cover of any description on the ramparts. The enemy had evidently been doubtful from the first, as to the manner in which their masonry would stand the heavy pounding of the French guns, or else they feared the splinters of stone, as they had shielded their embrasures and epaulements with many bales of linen, cotton, &c. These, however, were soon knocked away, and the epaulements became a shapeless heap of ruins. The besieged were, however, in no way disheartened, having a garrison of 2,000 picked men prepared for a most vigorous resistance. Nevertheless, by ten o'clock the enemy's fire ceased, and the French observed some 500 of the garrison quietly slip through the doorway and rush for the citadel. The fire from the Château de l'Empereur had been, as a rule, directed too high, and most of the cannon balls had gone over the trenches and had done no damage to the French. Shortly after ten o'clock the powder magazine in the round tower of the château exploded, and the besiegers in their trenches received some injury from a rain of falling stones, &c., blown up by the explosion. For a few minutes the besiegers were so surprised by the awfulness of the explosion that they took no steps to ascertain what had really occurred, but as the wind gradually blew the smoke away, the Château de l'Empereur emerged from its canopy, with the battlements looking much the same as before the upheaval, excepting that the squat tower or keep, used as the powder magazine, had disappeared. But from the left flank of the French position it was soon seen that though the front was practically uninjured, yet the explosion had blown a hole in that side of the château which looked towards that flank.

General Hurel, who was commanding the trenches, on learning of this breach at once ordered the supporting troops to move forward round the side of the château, and so to enter by this new-found road.

It was then found that the magazine had been blown up by the garrison. Apparently they were dissatisfied with the resistance which their stone walls were offering to the French cannonade, which was not as great as they had been led to expect, and, passing quickly from the highest confidence to the deepest

THE CONQUEST OF ALGERIA 53

despondency, had blown up the magazine in a fit of despair, hoping to overwhelm at least some of the French in the ruins.

The interior showed what damage had been wrought, in a large measure, by the French cannonade previous to the explosion of the magazine. Everywhere fragments of French shells lay about with heaps of broken masonry, and scattered everywhere were corpses and debris of human remains. The French immediately proceeded to place a battery of ten cannon in the château, and meanwhile turned three of the enemy's guns and two French field pieces on to one of the sea front forts. Its fire was promptly extinguished, as, owing to the great command of the captured work, the French had a great advantage. An attempted escalade of this fort, made with daring courage by the Grenadiers of the 35th Regiment of the Line, was, however, defeated by the garrison. In the town everything was in confusion. The Dey is reported to have sent orders to all the commanders of the various forts to resist to the uttermost, and then to blow up, each, his fort, rather than to let them fall into the hands of the infidel, adding that so long as his palace stood he would defend it, and would prefer to blow up the kasbah and all in it, rather than to surrender.

However, 'necessity' is a hard master, and so Hussein found, for nothing could now stand against the commanding position captured by the French. About two o'clock the Dey sent out a messenger with a white flag, conveying his wish to treat. His offers were rather ridiculous. They were, that he should apologise to the French Government for any insult offered to them, and that he should pay the cost of the war. The French general's reply was to demand that the citadel and all the forts should at once be handed over to him, otherwise he declined to negotiate at all. Shortly afterwards two Moors, who turned out to be the chief men of the city, arrived and cheerfully offered to bring the Dey's head on a plate to the French if they would promise not to enter the town. This also was refused. The Dey then sent to the French admiral, hoping to obtain better terms from him; but to his discomfort he was simply referred again to the French general. Then the English consul and vice-consul were pressed into the service, and sent out to try and obtain good terms for the city. Again the French general refused to negotiate excepting on his own terms. At last, convinced that their day of reckoning was come, the Turkish envoy asked for the exact terms demanded by the French. They were very simple: (1) That all the forts of Algiers should be handed over at ten o'clock next morning to the French; (2) That the Dey should have his liberty and all his possessions guaranteed, and that he might retire to any place he might fix, the same to apply to all the soldiers and militia; (3) The free exercise of the Mahomedan religion, and perfect freedom for all classes to be guaranteed, and their women to be kept from insult. There appeared to be some doubt at first if the regular soldiers of the Dey's army would allow their master to accept these terms, but he himself was most willing to do so, though he demanded that the time for handing over the forts should be changed from ten o'clock on the morning of the 5th July to the same hour on the 6th. The French

THE CONQUEST OF ALGERIA 55

consented to have the time extended to noon on the 5th, if the survivors of the crews of the two wrecked French brigs were set free at once; and thus matters were finally settled.

Large numbers of the inhabitants quitted the city during the night of the 4th-5th July by the roads leading south and east, or by boat. A few French soldiers managed to push in before the entrance of the main army, and stole various things from the Dey's apartments at the kasbah; but this disorder was soon stopped. The general who commanded the garrison in the Château de l'Empereur turned out to be the State Treasurer. He gravely handed over the key of the treasury to the French and showed them where the treasure was stored. They found a log laid on the ground in a vault, and behind it the gold coins were lying, all values mixed together. The total amount in the treasury was just under £2,000,000. This large sum was sufficient to pay all the expenses of the French expedition, and was all the more curious, for, as noted by Sir Lambert Playfair, the actual trade of the port of Algiers at that time did not exceed £175,000 per annum.

No doubt it was the result of years of saving and plundering: not only of the tribes in Algeria, but of the weaker European countries situated on the Mediterranean Sea.

At the 'mint' there was only some £1,000. A guard was placed over both places, but a hole was broken through the wall of the 'mint' during the night on the opposite side to the sentry, and all the money was stolen.

So fell Algiers. As M. de Bourmont well said in

his orders of the day, preserved by M. Rousset: 'Twenty days were sufficient for the destruction of this State, whose existence had oppressed Europe during three centuries.'

M. de Bourmont was right and wrong. Twenty days sufficed to conquer the Turks or governing race and to take their 'city.' It was twenty-seven years before Algeria, the 'State' referred to, was finally conquered; and even in 1872, forty years after this time, rebellion lifted its untamed head.

On the 10th of July the Dey embarked for Naples. He was conveyed on the frigate *Jeanne d'Arc*. His harem and relatives, &c., went with him, and the total party was 110 souls, exactly half of whom were women. He landed in Naples on the 31st of July. Hussein afterwards retired to Egypt, where he was received with great consideration by Mehemet Ali, the famous ruler of that State. It is reported, however, that his death occurred shortly after an interview with Mehemet Ali, and it was accompanied by every sign of poisoning.

On the 5th of July all the janizaries or regular Turkish soldiers had been directed to deposit their arms at the kasbah. Then it was decided that all the unmarried men of the corps should be sent into Asia Minor. The French punctiliously paid them two months' pay, and a certain amount for subsistence on the voyage. Two thousand five hundred men were at once dispatched to Smyrna on board of four men-of-war.

On the 18th of July arrived an order from the French king creating M. de Bourmont a marshal of France.

It is noted by French historians that, on the explosion of the powder magazine of the Château de l'Empereur, the Kabyles and Arabs, who had been waiting a favourable opportunity to attack the right flank of the French, immediately disappeared like rats leaving a sinking ship.

Apparently they thought, however, that the French would be satisfied with the capture of the city alone.

CHAPTER VI

AFTER the conquest of the city it became the task of the conquerors to arrange for the government of the place, and, if possible, for the ruling of the surrounding country which had belonged to the Dey. To carry on necessary government in the town now that the Turks were gone, they installed a committee of Moors, whilst the Jews, as before, remained a separate body under their own headman.

To rule the neighbouring tribes another Moor, named Sida Hamdan, a merchant, was appointed aga of the Arabs. The Arabs looked on the appointment of a despised Moor to rule them as a studied insult, and only waited their time to show their opinion. The Bey of Titteri, last commander-in-chief of the Dey's army, came in and surrendered on the 7th of July; and on the 15th of the same month was duly given back his beylik, on condition of remaining faithful to the French and paying to them the same tribute as he had paid to the Dey. The Bey of Oran was anxious to surrender too, as he was an old worn-out man, but the Bey of Constantine, Hadj Ahmed, appeared determined to hold out as an independent prince. He therefore settled himself down for three days on the right bank of the Harrach river and awaited the course of events. The French sent a regiment towards his position under the command of

THE CONQUEST OF ALGERIA 59

General Montlivault. Hadj Ahmed then decided to retire towards his own beylik of Constantine, and slowly withdrew, taking with him all the cattle and flocks he was able to lay hands upon, including the breeding stud of the Dey, which was noted for its splendid Arab breed of horses.

He retired across the mountains towards Constantine, passing through some defiles known as the 'Portes de Fer,' which are described later on in this work.

The sight of the immense droves of cattle, &c., was too great a trial for the robber inhabitants of these mountains, and they attacked him and captured the greater part of his ill-gotten booty.

Still he arrived at Constantine and established himself strongly there, and became an important enemy of the French later on.

The French Army was now concentrated at Algiers, Sidi Ferruch was abandoned, and all the vast stores from its depôt were brought into the city of Algiers. On the 22nd of July the Marshal sent out a small column to proceed to Blida. Blida is an inland town situated some thirty-two miles from Algiers. It now possesses a population of some 13,000, and was probably rather less in 1830. It was a Roman military station in ancient times, and was used for the same purpose by the Turks. Destroyed by an earthquake in A.D. 1825, it was promptly rebuilt, and was in a most flourishing condition at the time of the French invasion. Blida is surrounded by trees and rather prettily situated, and is known amongst the Arabs as 'Blida the voluptuous.'

The French column consisted of one battalion

of light infantry, eight rifle companies, one squadron of cavalry, some engineers, and a section of field artillery and one mountain gun. They moved out fourteen miles that evening, and on the 23rd, being joined by the Marshal, proceeded to Blida, where they bivouacked, being peacefully received by the inhabitants.

Next morning, the 24th of July, part of the force made a reconnaissance for some five miles beyond Blida, and were fired upon by the Kabyles. The first losses suffered, however, were those of two unfortunate non-commissioned officers of artillery, who were seized whilst watering their horses, and were promptly murdered. Other stragglers were also seized by the treacherous inhabitants, who promptly struck off their heads. The French, suspecting no harm after their peaceable reception by the people of Blida, had placed their main body in the suburbs, whilst their headquarters, with the Marshal, were quartered in the town. The Marshal had a very slender escort and it was sharply attacked, the first man to fall being his senior aide-de-camp, Major de Tulan, who was mortally wounded as he stepped out of the Marshal's front door. The headquarters party fought their way towards the main body, but would probably have been overwhelmed if they had not been reinforced by three extra companies, wisely dispatched to their assistance, from the main body of the French in the suburbs. Collecting his forces with some difficulty, the Marshal proceeded to retreat towards Algiers. The column was now surrounded by numerous bodies of men on foot, who fired without ceasing from every point of vantage, whilst on every side, as far as the eye could reach, rode mounted Arabs. The French steadily retreated, each arm supporting the other, the cavalry charging when necessary, and the infantry firing a volley, whilst the guns fired a round or two at the enemy whenever the others were hard pressed. As night fell, the enemy disappeared as by magic.

About eleven o'clock at night the column halted and bivouacked, and it was at this bivouac that Marshal Bourmont actually received his Marshal's bâton from the hands of the king's messenger. The troops regained Algiers next day, the 25th of July, having lost 15 killed and 43 wounded.

The next act of Marshal Bourmont was to send 1,000 married janizaries to Smyrna, as he was under the impression that they were fomenting disturbances amongst the inhabitants of the country. An expedition was now sent to Oran and to Boné; the one to Oran was recalled before landing, that to Boné landed peaceably, and was well received by the inhabitants of that town, but for three weeks fought daily skirmishes with Arabs and Kabyles alike, outside the gates. The town of Boné was inhabited by Moors or Mozabites, and was coveted by the Bey of Constantine, but the townspeople would have none of him. That French expedition was also recalled at the end of the twenty-one days, and the inhabitants were left to their own devices. Having been provided with ammunition by the French, the people of Boné prepared to hold their town against the enemy on the landward side, and the last sound heard by the French, as they embarked, was the guns of the place repulsing an attack on the town.

The reason of this hasty recall was that a revolution had occurred in France; Charles X was driven from his throne, and he left the Duke of Orleans in charge of the kingdom. The latter then allowed himself to be proclaimed King of France. Marshal Bourmont decided to leave 12,000 of his 30,000 men to hold Algeria, and to transport the remainder to France, to place them at the disposal of Charles X. The fleet, however, influenced by the admiral, declared for the new Government and refused to assist him.

The Government of the Duke of Orleans naturally requested the Marshal to give up the command of the French Army in Algeria, and sent Marshal Clauzel (who arrived in Algiers on the 2nd of September) to relieve him of his command. Naturally also, the natives of the country would not let such a favourable opportunity of revolting go by. And the Bey of Titteri from his capital at Medea wrote renouncing his allegiance.

Not content with renouncing his allegiance, he aspired to take over the whole kingdom which had fallen from the hand of the last Dey, Hussein. When summoned to come to Algiers to give an account of his province, he promptly replied that, if he came, it would be with 200,000 men at his back. He also proceeded to coin money, and issued a proclamation stating that he had been appointed Dey by the Sultan of Turkey, and that he was so recognised by the Emperor of Morocco. He further added significantly, that he had powder and bullets to last him for a war of ten years. In Algiers itself a traffic in arms was discovered from the town into the country. Two of the unfortunates engaged in this trade were tried by

THE CONQUEST OF ALGERIA 63

court-martial and shot. This prompt action discouraged the seditious for the time being, and the town and neighbourhood remained fairly peaceable. On the 17th of August the white flag of France was lowered and the tricolour hoisted in its place on the citadel of Algiers, by order of the new Government.

Marshal Bourmont handed over command of the army on the 3rd of September, and embarked the same evening. He had asked that he might leave in a man-of-war, but Admiral Duperré, who was always, though his colleague, bitterly opposed to him, refused to grant him permission to sail in one. The Marshal had therefore to leave in an Austrian trading brig, but, as the merchantman left the port, the batteries thundered out a salute, by order of Marshal Clauzel, his successor.

Shortly before his departure, he had formed a corps of native scouts, some 500 strong, of various tribes and peoples, both Kabyles and Arabs. A large number were drawn from a Kabyle tribe named Zaouaoua, and from this name came the title of Zouave, so well known in England during the Crimean War, and always the incarnation of soldierly pluck and dash.

CHAPTER VII

EARLY in October, the Bey of Titteri moved forward with his forces towards Algiers. A force sent by him in advance appeared in a place called Camp de l'Harrach. Two small columns of French were sent to turn him out, which they did without much trouble. This day the Zouaves received their baptism of fire, and behaved very gallantly.

A short account, abbreviated from M. Rousset's works, may be given here of the formation of the Zouaves. They were formed of all shades of natives: Coulouglis, Negroes, Arabs or Kabyles. Eight companies were ordered to be formed, but only three were organised. A fourth was in process of formation at the time of this engagement. Officers were obtained, by promising any French line officer a step in rank, with the further promise that, after two years' service with the Zouaves, he might rejoin his own corps in that advanced rank.

When the Bey of Titteri advanced, the Zouaves went out with one of the French columns, and formed the advanced guard. These unfortunate men were practically clothed in rags, coats of all descriptions being seen in their ranks. They hardly knew how to handle their arms, yet they clambered bravely forward up some crests of hills, which were lightly held by the enemy.

They were then ordered to drive off some twenty Arab horsemen, and when they proceeded to do so, these Arabs fell back first on some hundred others, and then on some 400 Arabs, who defended themselves stoutly in a fortified enclosure. Two howitzers were sent to support the Zouaves, and after a sharp musketry fight, the house was stormed with great gallantry by this newly-raised corps. From that time on the Zouaves came into favour, and have ever since been a *corps d'élite* in the French army.

Marshal Clauzel had been directed to send some troops to France, which he did; but weakened as he was by this order, he found it necessary to send an expedition to Medea to depose the Bey of Titteri, and to instal a new man in his place. Again a rich Moor, a merchant, was chosen for this post, a choice which, though the French did not know it, was most hateful to the Arabs, who looked down on the Moors as not being their equals, and who had a supreme contempt for trade. The force moved out 8,000 strong on the 17th of November, but of the whole number only some two squadrons of mounted troops were provided. The transport was equally meagre, consisting of 21 wagons and 300 pack mules.

The first halt was made at the farm of the Bey of Oran. Part of this march had been made through a swamp formed by the overflow of the Harrach river, which had made the day a very trying one. The 18th of November, under a heavy rain, the march to Blida was resumed. The Arabs and Kabyles attempted to make a stand in front of Blida, but the French force after a short action drove them off, escaladed the walls, and took the town. Next morning the skirmishing continued, and whilst the cavalry engaged the Arabs in the plain, and the infantry burnt and destroyed crops and huts over three or four miles of the mountains, the camp followers plundered Blida, whilst the gendarmes who accompanied the column tried to stop them. Any native taken with arms was at once shot by the French. The inhabitants of Blida, who had fled to the hills before the arrival of the French, came in on the evening of the 19th and made their submission. They asserted that the Kabyles had compelled them to leave the town, so as to avoid meeting their friends, the French.

On the 20th of November the column halted at Haouch Mouzaia. Here two chiefs of Arab tribes came in and asked to be confirmed in their appointments by the French, and warned the French general that the Bey of Titteri proposed to fight at Tenia de Mouzaia, a pass in the mountains before arriving at Medea.

Marshal Clauzel then left his wagons and field guns, with a regiment to protect them, and next day pushed forward to the fight. The ground became very rough, and large masses of Kabyles, unarmed, stood on the hills watching them. About midday a single shot rang out, and promptly all the peaceable Kabyles reappeared with arms in their hands. The two surrendered Arab tribes also attacked the French, whilst the men of the Bey of Titteri manfully bore their part in an attack on the French advanced guard. The French turned the enemy's flanks and also assailed them in front, scrambling up precipices and down into ravines.

THE CONQUEST OF ALGERIA 67

Finally all the enemy were swept away. The pass was found to be a cutting in the rocks some seven feet wide only. The first Frenchman who reached the top was Lieutenant MacMahon, a soldier well known in French history, sometimes in misfortune, but always full of courage. The French lost 220 men killed and wounded at this attack. Leaving a brigade on the pass and sending some men to burn the huts of the two treacherous Arab tribes, the general then pushed on towards Medea on the 22nd of November, with some six battalions and the cavalry. That evening the French entered Medea. The inhabitants surrendered the town to them, and even assisted to chase away the Arabs and Kabyles who hung about.

Medea appeared to be a cheerful little walled town with a citadel, &c. The population was some 6,000 people, and it stood on a rock some 3,000 feet above sea level.

The population of this town is much reduced in numbers since the French occupation. It is now just under 4,000 souls. It is supposed to stand on the site of the old Roman town of 'Mediæ,' so called from being half-way between two, somewhat more important, Roman military stations. It is sixty-three miles from Algiers, and is surrounded by a wall with five gates in it.

Next day the Bey of Titteri came in and surrendered. The French general then decided to leave a small garrison at Medea. He sent fifty mounted men of the artillery to Algiers to bring out a supply of cartridges. It will be remembered that Marshal Clauzel took but very little transport with him on this expedition. The result was that very little spare ammunition could be carried. After the severe fighting he had gone through, his column was very short of ammunition. Still, as he preferred to leave a garrison in Medea, it was absolutely necessary to leave them some reserve of ammunition. This reserve could only be formed by collecting ammunition from the pouches of the infantry of the column. By the greatest exertions a reserve of 20,000 cartridges was left in Medea. Each infantryman of the retreating column had thus left in his possession twenty cartridges. There was absolutely no other reserve of ammunition of any sort with the column. The garrison's treasury at Medea was filled in almost as curious a manner as the ammunition magazine. The Bey of Titteri having surrendered, his conquerors borrowed what money he could spare from him, and formed it into a treasury chest for the garrison. It only amounted to some £400, but it was all that could be obtained at the moment.

The small party of artillerymen dispatched to Algiers was attacked by the Arabs and annihilated. On the 26th of November the French retired from Medea. They were not molested. Near Blida, however, on the 27th they met the enemy, who fled on their approach. At Blida they found that the French garrison had had a hard struggle for their lives. The Kabyles had attacked the town from the 20th of November, and being admitted by the inhabitants on the 25th, had remained hidden in the houses until the 26th, when at daybreak they fell upon the French in the town, assisted by the treacherous townsmen, whilst other large bodies of Kabyles had attacked from

THE CONQUEST OF ALGERIA 69

outside. Still the French had won, and the inhabitants had perished in large numbers under the bayonets of the French and under the knives of their allies, the Kabyles.

The French moved slowly back to Algiers, arriving there on the 29th of November, protecting a large crowd of inhabitants, principally Jews, with women and children flying from Blida. They passed the whole of the fifty massacred artillerymen, whose bodies were disgracefully mangled, and also the body of a poor female canteen keeper hung to a tree by the feet. In the meantime Medea had been repeatedly attacked by the Kabyles. The fighting continued until the 30th of November, when a heavy rain drove the attackers back to their mountains, to the great relief of the French, who were running short of cartridges. The French lost 190 killed and wounded during this fighting at Medea.

They were supplied with fresh cartridges in a very curious manner. These cartridges were made up at Algiers in bales representing cloths, &c. They were then given, by the usual merchants, to some Arab tribe, who made a business of guarding convoys, to transport to Medea, which they duly did, being unaware of the contents of their bales of merchandise. Possibly some of the same tribe were taking part in the attack on Medea, thus revealing a curious state of affairs and different interests in the country.

On the 7th of December 1830, after a week of heavy rain, an expedition was sent under General Boyer, bringing food, money, and further ammunition, to the French at Medea. The weather was awful, and included heavy snowstorms. On the 10th of

December the force duly arrived at Medea. On the 12th the rain at last ceased, and, leaving a new garrison, the French column took its way by the Tenia de Mouzaia to Algiers, and was nearly overwhelmed by a further dreadful snowstorm on the mountains.

Now a curious interlude occurred. France, threatened at home with European troubles, directed that all her army of occupation in Algeria, but 10,000 men, should be sent home. The Marshal, at his wits' end to keep the conquest with all the troops he now had, knew that it would be impossible with those he would then be left with, so he increased the native troops in French pay, and handed over the Bey of Constantine's beylik and that of Oran to the Bey of Tunis, on condition of an annual tribute to the French Government. Also, he decided to withdraw the French garrison from Medea. This was done with the help of a brigade sent from Algiers. They left the men of Medea well supplied with arms and ammunition, and these latter bravely determined to give a good account of themselves against the Bey of Constantine or the Kabyles of the mountains.

On the 21st of February 1831, Marshal Clauzel returned to France, General Berthezene being sent from there as his successor. The French Government had disapproved of Marshal Clauzel's handing over Constantine and Oran to the Bey of Tunis, so these two places reverted nominally to the French. As a matter of fact, Constantine was held for himself for another six years by its own Turkish Bey, whilst Oran was handed over to the French on the first opportunity by its governor.

CHAPTER VIII

FRANCE was in no very good condition at this particular time to carry on the war with Africa.

She had just passed through a revolution and change of dynasties at home, and everything was in a most unsettled state not only in Belgium but in Spain. A general opinion prevailed in Europe that she should have permitted the affairs of Algeria to be settled by a congress of European Powers. In fact, Colonel Scott, writing in his diary shortly after this time, states that France had given such a promise. However that may have been, her ministers were none too pleased to find an indefinite guerilla war thrust on their hands; and to add to their troubles, Lord Aberdeen interviewed the French ambassador at the Court of St. James, and warned him in the most solemn manner that England had great grievances against France over this question. No one appears to have realised that Europe was deeply indebted to France for rooting out such a nest of anarchy, and all these considerations must be taken into account by the reader, when he wonders why France did not bend herself to the work of conquest in a whole-hearted manner, instead of in the desultory way in which she now appeared to act.

But to return to the new Governor of Algeria. General Berthezene had been in Africa before, viz.

at the taking of Algiers. He considered it his duty to make various military marches through the neighbouring country, and on the 1st of March 1831, took some 8,000 men through the country by Blida and Kolea.

The latter place, Kolea, is one of the sacred towns of Algeria. It is some twenty-five miles from Algiers, and has a population of nearly 5,000 inhabitants. The sacredness of the place appears to arise from a Mahomedan saint, named Ali-ben-Embark, having lived there A.D. 1625, and his descendants also resided there in 1831. His first claim to fame arose from the fact that, though given to sleeping whilst he should have been working, yet, owing to his sanctity, the work went on just as well, whether he were asleep or awake. His master discovered him asleep whilst his oxen obediently ploughed the ground as if he were guiding them. Nothing more was needed to prove his saintliness in a simple-minded countryman's brain, and his reputation was established. He inherited his master's property in the town at that master's death. There is also at Kolea a tomb of one of the last representatives of the kings of Numidia, Juba II. His daughter, Drusilla, is more widely known than her father, as she was the wife of the Roman Governor Felix, who was the unjust judge before whom St. Paul appeared, and who wrongfully detained him in custody for two years.

In the meantime, some of the leading natives who were in friendly relations with the French in the surrounding country were assassinated. On the 7th of May yet again General Berthezene paraded the country, demanding reparation for the assassination

THE CONQUEST OF ALGERIA

of these men, and the delivery to him of the assassins. All he received, however, was that his stragglers were cut off pitilessly by his stealthy enemy.

Towards the end of June the new Bey of Titteri, who was established in Medea, sent in word that he was hard pressed, as the eldest son of the late Bey had raised a force and was occupying the country near the town, and preventing provisions from being brought in as usual by the country people.

General Berthezene took 4,500 men, of whom only two squadrons of cavalry formed part, and marched on the 25th of June to the assistance of Medea. He made a serious mistake in taking only forty-five cartridges per man. Arriving at Medea, he went out on the 1st of July with three columns to destroy crops and villages belonging to the enemy. The enemy appeared in great numbers on the hills, but retired as he advanced. When his turn came to retire, however, the enemy advanced and boldly attacked him. After he re-entered Medea, great numbers of tribesmen poured off the hills towards the town, evidently under the impression that the victory was theirs.

The General then decided to evacuate the town. Many inhabitants obtained permission to retire with the column, including the Bey, who resigned his functions. The column moved off in the afternoon of the 2nd of July, and marched away under a continual fire from the enemy. When they halted for the night, information was obtained from some Arab spies that the enemy proposed to rush the camp at midnight. Leaving the fires burning, the French moved quietly off at eleven o'clock. Passing through the Tenia de Mouzaia, the enemy rushed in on the French troops, and for a moment a panic occurred. Soon, however, it was stopped by the Zouaves and the 67th Regiment of the Line, assisted by a detachment of various corps, which body made a most brave resistance in a hand-to-hand struggle. A mountain gun would have been lost, only a brave artillery captain defended it single-handed with his sword. A Major Duvivier bravely returned and drove off the enemy and brought off the gun in triumph.

At Haouch Mouzaia, where the troops halted at the end of their night march, they found that their wily enemy had stopped up the stream which supplied the place with water, and all that day they had to remain in bivouac, dying of thirst. The enemy moved down the road towards Algiers, and held the ford of the Chiffa in overwhelming numbers. Warned of this, the General moved away to the westward some six miles at nightfall, and crossed by another ford. On the 5th of July the troops regained Algiers, having lost in the expedition some 400 killed and wounded.

The net result of these operations was that the whole country rose in revolt; at the same time some 3,000 of the small French force were in hospital with fever. The flocks of the garrison were carried off, many men were murdered outside the lines, and at least one within them. From the 15th to the 20th of July a small French column was busy driving off the enemy, who attacked every blockhouse or detached party with great bitterness. On the 20th, for instance, they were so daring that they attacked 400 men of

THE CONQUEST OF ALGERIA 75

the 67th Regiment, who fled, losing thirty-five killed and wounded. Relief came to the French, however, more from the needs of the enemy than from any effective results of their column movements. On the 22nd of July the enemy had disappeared. They were known to have gone to their homes for further provisions, ammunition, &c., as always happens in the case of such irregular volunteers, as Prince Charles Stuart found to be the case, to his cost, with his Highlanders in 1745.

In May 1831, the inhabitants of the coast town of Boné, always fairly friendly to the French, sent to them for assistance, as they were closely blockaded by their old enemy, the Bey of Constantine, and by the Kabyles. The General sent 130 of the Zouaves with some junior, or 'company' officers. Major Herder and Captain Bigot accompanied these forces. On arrival Major Herder weakly left the force badly placed, and, in fact, took no steps for the security of the place. In the meantime a Coulouglis, named Sidi Ahmed, who up to now had been chief of the forces of the town, decided to rid himself of these Europeans. This man had originally only been in charge of some 100 Turks or Coulouglis, but being of a stirring nature had made himself very useful to the people in the town in the defence of the place, and he now aspired to make himself the ruler of the town, and as much land outside of it as he could seize. Naturally, the arrival of French troops interfered with his plans. He had hoped for arms, money, and ammunition to be sent, perhaps native volunteers to serve in his ranks; not French officers and their men. Besides Ahmed, however, there was another man named Ibrahim, who was much more dangerous to the French. He had at one time been the Bey of Constantine, and he wormed himself into the confidence of the French officers. By arrangement with Ahmed, the 25th of September 1831 was decided upon as the day to commence the attack on the French soldiers. The officers lived in the most complete security, and it was not, therefore, very difficult to take them by surprise. Ibrahim's chief anxiety was to seize the citadel. It was only garrisoned by a few of the Zouaves, and the doors were left open; so when Ibrahim presented himself there, followed by some fifty men, little or no resistance was made. A few men, who might have given trouble, were bought off by small presents of money, and the officer in charge of the citadel having gone into the town to breakfast, nothing remained to be done but to put the disarmed French troops outside, and to shut the door of the kasbah upon them.

The preconcerted signal for the rising had been the sailing of the French corvette, named the *Creole*, which vessel was taking dispatches from Boné to Algiers. So soon as the kasbah was taken, it was arranged that three cannon should be fired as a signal that it was in Ibrahim's hands, and that then the French should be attacked wherever they might happen to be in the town. The three cannon were duly discharged, but they had one unlooked-for result. This unusual noise brought the corvette, and a French brig with her, back to the anchorage. During two days the Zouaves, reinforced by 100 marines landed from the French ships-of-war, made head against all attacks; but at last the Turks, reinforced by some Kabyles from outside, drove them out, and some fifty Zouaves only were able to join the French ships. Some others surrendered and joined the insurgents, and some thirty were made prisoners. Captain Bigot covered the French retreat, and, his men of the rear guard being struck down around him, gallantly devoted his own life to cover the retreat of the main body. Alone in a narrow passage he stood at bay, and, when rushed by the enemy, killed two before he was struck down himself by a musket shot. He was promptly cut to pieces.

Major Herder was one of the last to leave the shore, and, being hard pressed and wounded, threw himself into the sea and swam to one of the ships. He was unfortunately killed by a bullet through the head as he reached the French vessel.

The French ships cannonaded the town, but the cannonade ceased when a deputation of the inhabitants arrived to point out that they were forced to join these people, and did not do so willingly.

On the 30th of September another 200 Zouaves, under Major Duvivier, arrived, and he was most anxious to land and to take the town; but the naval commander, perhaps wisely, refused to risk his ships in the encounter, and the whole force returned to Algiers.

To the west the French had Oran garrisoned by the 21st Regiment of the Line. For some reason this unfortunate regiment appeared to be forgotten, and received no pay, clothing, &c., and the officers were little better off than the men. The town of Oran also hardly ever received communications from outside: sometimes two months passed in this manner;

so on the whole, life at Oran was not very pleasant for the French soldiers. The Governor of Oran, appointed by the Bey of Tunis in accordance with his arrangements with Marshal Clauzel, duly arrived there, but finding everything more or less impoverished did not seem much impressed with this new acquisition of his master's. However, he was a man of action, and finding that some tribes refused to acknowledge him as governor, he promptly visited them, killed some forty tribesmen, and returned home in triumph with a great spoil of cattle and sheep, &c.

In the meantime, as already stated, the Bey of Tunis and the French Government could not agree as to the terms on which Tunis should hold the beylik of Oran, so the native governor gladly returned to Tunis. The French then found that though the people about Oran had not shown any particular regard for the Tunisian governor, they strongly objected to the French as their masters, and the local markets were deserted, and the cattle belonging to the garrison were also driven off, and life became even harder than it had been, in this unsatisfactory town. All its Mahomedan inhabitants had already left, and only Jews remained.

The French commanders were changed from time to time. One was General Boyer, who had been in the Egyptian campaign with the Great Napoleon, and had then served under Mahomet Ali; and yet again had been in Spain from 1810 to 1813. Of a stern disposition, he was hated by the Spaniards, and the natives of Oran had heard tales of his great severity which frightened them. His proceedings certainly justified the popular idea, for,

THE CONQUEST OF ALGERIA 79

seizing some Moorish merchants supposed to be in communication with the Emperor of Morocco's troops, he calmly directed them to be beheaded without trial, and hanged a spy, and the crew of a vessel caught selling powder to the natives, also without any trial.

During this time further reinforcements arrived for Oran, increasing the garrison from some 1,400 to 2,000 men, and the Moors, who had tried to carry Mostaganem by assault, were repulsed by the Coulouglis, who held not only that place but also Tlemcen. Also two very powerful Arab tribes, named Douair and Sméla, made friendly overtures, so, on the whole, things appeared to be brightening for the practically blockaded garrison of Oran.

The two towns referred to as held by the Coulouglis, Mostaganem and Tlemcen, deserve some slight remark in passing. Mostaganem now has a population of some 14,000 souls. It was probably a good deal smaller in A.D. 1831. It had been a Roman port in ancient times, but an earthquake had destroyed its harbour. It again became important in the sixteenth century, and had a population of some 40,000 people. In A.D. 1558 the Spaniards tried to take the town, but it successfully resisted all their attacks; but its prosperity waned from this time on.

Tlemcen was even more important than Mostaganem. Its population, now about 23,000, was also less in 1831. Originally known as Pomaria by the Romans on account of the flourishing fruit trees, it became the capital of an Arab kingdom, and about the time of our Norman Conquest, or a little later, it numbered 150,000 people. It consisted of two towns within a stone's throw of one another. In A.D. 1300 it was besieged by a rival Arab power, and the siege lasted eight years; but the city did not surrender, and the siege had to be raised. Many other vicissitudes befell the town before the period of which we now speak—too many to be dealt with here.

About this time the French Government decided to send General Savary to Algeria to replace General Berthezene, and, at the same time, efforts were made to increase the French forces, despite the withdrawal of line regiments. Various means were tried, besides raising native troops. For instance, an African Light Infantry was formed out of the malefactors of the army, and acquitted themselves better than might have been expected. Another means taken was to send culprits actually under sentence to a 'disciplinary company' in Africa, instead of putting them into prison in France; whilst another corps, known as the Foreign Legion, was raised from any foreigner willing to enlist who appeared capable of fighting. The officers of these corps must have been men of great determination and strength of character. One French officer mentions that he noticed a company of the Foreign Legion, all of whom were drunk, and who celebrated the glad occasion by beating all their officers and non-commissioned officers. That they did not do so unrewarded is, however, also made plain, as the same officer mentions that all the company were safely lodged in gaol, and two were duly tried by court-martial with more than serious results to themselves.

THE CONQUEST OF ALGERIA

They were of many nationalities. Colonel Scott mentions that forty Spaniards came over to the Arabs once in a body, as deserters from the Foreign Legion, after shooting their officers. Again, at the siege of Constantine, the 'Memoirs of the Duc d'Orleans' state that previous to the assault the Duc de Nemours incited the Foreign Legion then present to the attack, by a stirring address in German; whilst in some of the actions—the province of Oran and elsewhere—we find that the Poles formed whole companies in the Foreign Legion. Like Hereward the Wake, they fought desperately for the freedom of their own country, but spent their spare time in assisting to enslave another people.

The 'Chasseurs d'Afrique' also came into being at that time, two squadrons being formed from volunteers from the 12th Chasseurs who were desirous of remaining in Africa, whilst natives were enlisted and put in, to fill up the ranks.

CHAPTER IX

ONE of General Savary's first acts was to establish his Algiers garrison in entrenched posts some miles from Algiers, leaving only one regiment in the town. He also greatly improved the hospital accommodation for the troops. His next act is greatly to his discredit. An embassy from Biskra—an oasis with five villages situated to the south-west of Constantine —after being entertained most hospitably at Algiers, was attacked and robbed near the latter town whilst returning home by some insignificant Arab tribe. General Savary immediately sent out a body of troops and surrounded the tents or wretched huts of these people, and massacred all the men, some seventy in number, including two deserters from the Foreign Legion. Worse followed, however, for four men were brought back as prisoners and tried by court-martial. Then it came out that this unfortunate tribe had had NOTHING to do with this particular theft. The court-martial were not desirous of acquitting the prisoners, on the curious ground that it would thus make clear to the world the great miscarriage of justice which had already taken place. So they convicted them and recommended them to mercy. Two of the prisoners managed to break out of prison; the other two were duly shot by General Savary's orders. Naturally

THE CONQUEST OF ALGERIA 83

the Arabs retaliated by an ambuscade, and twenty of the Foreign Legion were done to death.

A small expedition of 1,600 men was sent out on the 1st of October 1832 to attack an Arab camp near Boufarik. The march took place at night, and during the night the Arabs moved up towards the approaching French, with the result that they fell over one another at 3 a.m. The Arabs recovered from their surprise more quickly than the French, and opened a heavy fire, which put the Chasseurs d'Afrique to flight. They in turn broke the Zouaves, who were drawn up in square by their excellent Major, Duvivier. However, all rallied well, especially the Zouaves, and drove the Arabs off. They again attacked the column that afternoon as it was returning, with both horse and foot, but this time a dashing charge of the Chasseurs d'Afrique laid a hundred of the enemy dead on the ground. The total French loss was only twenty-one killed and wounded.

An expedition was also sent to Kolea and Blida —the first in October and the second in November. Contributions were levied on both towns, but they were not paid, excepting £300 from Kolea. Blida was pillaged by the troops and its walls blown up in places.

In A.D. 1832 General Savary, by means of a safe conduct addressed to a friendly Arab chief, was able to seize the persons of two other chiefs, who were distinctly unfriendly to the French; and in February 1833 he had them brought before a court-martial, and they were executed. In conjunction with his massacre at the miserable Arab village, this treacherous act did the French much harm. The despair of the Arab chief, who had unwittingly been used as a decoy to capture the other two unfriendly chiefs, was very real and very great. He repeatedly begged to be executed instead of the two captives, and altogether bore himself like a brave and honest man.

During 1832, also, the French recovered Boné under exciting circumstances. Besieged by the Bey of Constantine, the Turk Ibrahim who had seized the castle and turned the French out, as before narrated, now found that both he and the population of Boné were likely to starve. So they both had the impudence to again apply to the French for assistance. The French general replied in a friendly letter, that if Ibrahim was driven out, he could have an asylum with the French. He also sent some food, and a couple of adventurous officers, with a small ship to Boné. Then various negotiations went on. In the meantime the Bey of Constantine's army took the town, though not the citadel, where Ibrahim still reigned with a guard of Turks.

The French steadily negotiated with both parties. The Turks in the citadel revolted and turned Ibrahim out, and decided to allow thirty French sailors into the citadel. The only way of entry was by a rope, all other means of ingress being cut off by the Kabyles of the Bey of Constantine. The army of the Bey, seeing the citadel in possession of the French, and the town under fire from the guns of the citadel on one side, and from the guns of the ship on the other, withdrew into the country, taking all the inhabitants with them by force.

The Turks now in the citadel again revolted

THE CONQUEST OF ALGERIA

against the French garrison of thirty men, as they wished to be allowed to go down and pillage the empty town. Being much more numerous, they would have been most dangerous but for the promptitude of the French officer named Jusuf, who tried and shot three Turks, and arrested three others, and sent them down the rope to be confined in the French ship which still lay in the harbour. News of these successes having been received at Algiers, a French regiment was sent as a garrison, with some artillery and engineers, and the place was duly put into a good state of defence. Gradually, the wretched inhabitants, who were still alive, made their way back, and the town resumed its usual appearance.

The French began to make small expeditions from Boné with a view of clearing the surrounding country of active enemies. This was most necessary, as otherwise it became impossible for any of the neighbouring tribes who might be willing to do so, to bring in sheep or grain to the markets, as they were pounced upon either going or returning by other hostile clans. On the 28th of June 1832 one of the most powerful Arab tribes received such a lesson that they hurriedly retired towards the south. In September the Turk Ibrahim again appeared upon the scene at the head of 1,500 native warriors. He was attacked promptly by the French, and his army scattered. He vanished from the scene for ever from now on, as he was shortly after his defeat assassinated by order of the Bey of Constantine.

Towards the end of November a sort of yellow fever broke out in Boné, and for two months raged unchecked. All suffered alike natives and Europeans.

When it finally ceased, it was found that one quarter of the troops and of the inhabitants of the town had been carried off by this dreadful scourge. Undismayed, the French poured in more troops into the town, and the troops were so well used by the governor that friendly relations between the nearest tribes and the town were at last established.

CHAPTER X

AND now we come to a most notable event in the history of the French Conquest, i.e. the rise of Abd-el-Kader. Before, however, considering this, it would be well to reflect upon the position of the French and their great mistake, which mistake gave Abd-el-Kader the opportunity which he was not slow to seize. The French had now been more than two years in Algeria, and practically held only Algiers Boné, and Oran. They had succeeded the Turks in possession of these three towns, but had not taken up the rule the Turks had laid down in the surrounding provinces.

The French Home Government acted in an undecided manner, and did not see that up to now they had managed to hold their own in Algeria more on account of the divisions of Turks, Arabs, and Kabyles than on account of their troops' hard fighting. They continued their hesitating career as if utterly oblivious that it *was* possible for the people of Algeria to be united on one point at least, and that was, 'hatred' to the Christians if a 'holy war' should really be proclaimed. And this now came to pass.

Near Mascara, in the province of Oran, lived a marabout or Mahomedan saint, a descendant of the prophet named Mahi-ed-Dine. His family had originally come from Medina, had settled in Morocco, and then emigrated again to Mascara, where it had allied itself with the most powerful Arab tribe of Oran, the Hachem. This notable personage proclaimed a holy war against the infidel, and as he was too old to take the field, he sent his three sons to act for him, of whom the youngest, Abd-el-Kader, was chosen chief. He was twenty-four years of age in 1832, of middle height, very active, a good rider, and a clever speaker; in fact, a man of exceptional ability and courage.

Affairs in the Beylik of Oran were as follows. The garrison of Oran was some 2,500 men, of whom over 500 were good cavalry. Tlemcen was garrisoned by some Coulouglis (half-bred Turks), who held the town for themselves against the country people, who were aided by some forces of the empire of Morocco. Mostaganem was held by some Turks and Coulouglis in the pay of France. France further sent supplies of powder, &c., to Tlemcen to assist them in resisting attack, though they were not at the time submitted to France. The remainder of the country tribes spent their leisure in thieving forays against each other.

Such was the state of affairs as found by Abd-el-Kader. He commenced operations by attacking 100 French infantry with 400 Arabs. The infantry were rescued by the remainder of the garrison of Oran, after losing 15 killed and wounded out of their 100 men. This event occurred in April 1832. From the 2nd to the 9th of May, Oran was attacked by Abd-el-Kader, his father, and an army of the faithful. At one time their numbers exceeded 12,000 men. They

THE CONQUEST OF ALGERIA 89

were, however, beaten back, Abd-el-Kader losing his nephew in this attack.

On the 11th of October they again appeared, but only some 4,000 strong; but this time the French troops went to meet them instead of remaining in their forts, and they were easily put to flight.

The French at Oran, towards the middle of June, seized Arzeu, a small port to the east of Oran, sending stores by sea, and marching a column to it by land. The reason of this move was that the inhabitants, being friendly to the French and having sold them amongst other things some remounts for their cavalry, had felt the heavy hand of Abd-el-Kader. He seized the sheik of the town and had him led to Mascara, where he was strangled. It is interesting to note that Arzeu was of much assistance to the English during the Peninsular War, as many as 300 cargoes of grain being sent to them yearly from this port.

Various petty skirmishes went on between Abd-el-Kader and the French, in which the French always repelled all attacks, though sometimes losing a few killed and wounded. The chief sufferers were, of course, the neighbouring tribes, who were hounded on to fight by Abd-el-Kader, and who, when they fought with the French, were invariably beaten, and lost their flocks and herds as well. The French also in August occupied Mostaganem, which had been defended by the Turks in their name, and beat off a determined attack of Abd-el-Kader upon it during the first few days of that month, and as a counter-stroke made a raid on the neighbouring tribes, capturing eighty or ninety prisoners, but they were very severely harassed in their retirement. The Chasseurs d'Afrique especially behaved exceedingly well in this affair, but mutinied three weeks later in Oran, which mutiny was quelled with some difficulty.

In December 1833 some 2,500 French beat up Abd-el-Kader's camp in the plains, and after taking some prisoners from his allies, retired in good order into Oran.

In the meantime the French general now at Oran, named Desmichels, had been instructed from Paris to make a treaty of peace with Abd-el-Kader, if possible. He was directed to make him acknowledge the sovereignty of France, and that he was then to leave him in charge of several tribes in the interior. Instead of this the French general, most anxious to make the peace at any price, made a treaty as with an independent sovereign, whereby the French kept two officers as agents in Mascara, whilst Abd-el-Kader kept agents in Oran, Arzeu, and Mostaganem.

Even to this treaty the wily chief would not affix his seal until he received several other assurances from General Desmichels, which were kept secret, such as various restrictions on markets, &c., which, with astonishing foolishness, were placed under the charge of Abd-el-Kader's agents, and could only be held at certain places as he wished, whilst powder, &c., must be supplied to him by the French.

This able man thus established himself as ruler in the interior, drew a rent from the French markets, and, when the neighbouring tribes rose against his demands for tribute, he was able to crush them by the help of warlike stores drawn from the French. The Arab tribe called Douair in particular attacked

THE CONQUEST OF ALGERIA 91

him suddenly after refusing to pay tribute, and after fighting bravely, and having two horses killed under him, the Emir, as Abd-el-Kader was often called, had to fly, only to return a little later well supplied from France with 400 new muskets and barrels of powder to take vengeance on these 'rebels.'

He established himself at the town of Mascara, which he made his capital. It has a population of some 15,000 people at the present time, and according to the diary of Colonel Scott, who was there about the time we are speaking of, it had exactly the same population at that time. It was built on the site of an old Roman town.

Abd-el-Kader, though receiving presents of powder and muskets from France, decided to start factories for himself, and with the help of a Spaniard named Don Jose, from Andalusia, he was able to establish arsenals in various places. He also availed himself of the treaty of peace with France to import workmen from Paris for various purposes. He brought one man named De Casse from France, who smelted iron ore and cast various articles for him. The same French gentleman made some congreve rockets for the Emir, but something went wrong in the manufacture, and the rockets exploded unexpectedly, and nearly blew up the whole of Abd-el-Kader's staff. De Casse also projected a cloth factory, but this never came to perfection, as he caught fever and died before he could get it into working order. Other French workmen were employed in the works, and when these arsenals were working at their highest pitch they turned out some eight muskets per diem. All these workmen were well treated and well paid, and were duly sent to their homes in France by the Emir, at the expiration of their contract, with presents of money. Marshal Soult had such an admiration for this chieftain that he is known to have remarked that there were then only three great men living, and they were all Mahomedans. The three he meant were Abd-el-Kader, Mahomet Ali, Pasha of Egypt, and Schamyl, the heroic opponent of the Russians in the Caucasus.

It is now necessary to see what was passing elsewhere in Algeria at this time.

CHAPTER XI

THE Duc de Rovigo, General Savary, died in the middle of 1833, and was succeeded in command by a General Voirol, who was a discreet person. He gathered the harvest round Algiers, and made roads, &c., about the place. He also sent out a few minor expeditions.

In the meantime a seaport named Bougie, possessing some 3,000 inhabitants, came into notice for a short time. Some insult had been offered to an English merchant vessel, and it was considered advisable by the Government in France to take over the town. The townspeople would not accept French protection, as they were threatened by the Kabyle hillsmen if they did so; and as Algiers could not spare any soldiers for the expedition, owing to the ravages of fever in the garrison, an expedition of eight war vessels and 1,800 soldiers was sent from Toulon. The fleet arrived on the 29th of September 1833, and the shore defences were at once engaged, their cannon fire being quickly silenced by the French sailors. The infantry then landed, and soon found that hard fighting was in front of them, as the Kabyles had occupied gardens, streets, hedges, &c., everywhere. The troops employed on this expedition were quite unused to war, having been taken from peaceful garrison work; but they did their best, and after two days' fighting, assisted by some mountain guns and a landing party from the fleet, succeeded in driving the Kabyles out of the town.

The tribesmen then took up their position on the hill outside Bougie, which hill rather overhung the town. The French tried to carry this camp on the night of the 2nd of October, but after some fighting were repulsed. Judging from their losses at this attack on the camp—seventeen killed and wounded—the troops could not have been very first rate. Fortunately, some reinforcements came up from Algiers, of seasoned troops, and a week of rain having been lived through, the French went out, and after eleven hours' fighting carried the enemy's camp in good style.

It is worth remarking that, in the first attack, the young French troops shot their Moorish guide, mistaking him for a Kabyle. They consoled themselves for his loss by recalling that during the fighting in the town he had killed fourteen women and children belonging to an ancient enemy, and thus unwittingly justice was satisfied.

The expedition had so far been commanded by a General Trézel. He had been hit by a bullet during the fighting, and after it was over returned to France to be cured. Major Duvivier was sent specially from France to command at Bougie. His garrison consisted of two regular battalions of the French line, two companies of the African Light Infantry, and four companies of the Zouaves.

During 1834 General Voirol at Algiers sent out and well punished a strong Arab tribe some forty-five miles from Algiers. It was considered a very

THE CONQUEST OF ALGERIA 95

strong tribe, as it could put 600 mounted men into the field. By dint of clever diplomacy two smaller Arab clans, who had suffered heavily from their stronger neighbours, assisted in the expedition, and behaved most bravely in action. Very large booty was taken, and was most sensibly handed over to the auxiliary Arabs. At Boné the French more than held their own, as the Bey of Constantine, by his cruelties, drove his own co-religionists over to the French for protection. For instance, one Arab tribe, having refused to pay tribute to him, was asked to come under a safe conduct to join in an attack on the infidel at Boné. During the first night the remainder of the Bey's forces were directed to attack, and kill, the men of this tribe. Some hundreds (more than half) were thus murdered; the remainder naturally fled for protection to the French. At the same time, life at Boné was none of the most healthy and pleasant, for during two months of the summer of 1833, 300 men died, whilst 1,600 were in hospital out of 2,400 of the garrison.

About this time, 1834, the French Government fixed 21,000 men as the permanent garrison of Algeria, to which number they proposed to add the native troops of all sorts.

General Voirol returned to France in December 1834, as Count d'Erlon had been sent as Governor-General of Algeria. This officer, Count d'Erlon, had fought at Waterloo, and it will be remembered that two days previous to that famous battle, he had spent the afternoon industriously, marching from Quatre Bras to Ligny, and back again, in obedience to the orders of Napoleon, and Marshal Ney, alternately. He was now sixty-nine years of age. On arrival in Algiers he found that his garrison was 31,000 strong, not 21,000 as had been fixed. He further sent out the usual small expeditions from Algiers to punish the neighbouring tribes, which expeditions came to nothing as usual. He also found that the Kabyles at Bougie were full of fight, and daily attacking the French outposts. But, worst of all, he found that Abd-el-Kader had pushed into the Beylik of Titteri and had taken Miliana and Medea, and had drawn all the tribes round these towns into a treaty with him, and that he was even contemplating an expedition to Constantine. The Emir then sent to demand from the French at Oran two mortars to assist him in reducing the Coulouglis at Tlemcen. The French general, then Trézel, the conqueror of Bougie, promptly refused them. Abd-el-Kader directed the three great tribes near Oran to break off all communications with the French. The Douair and the Sméla refused to do so; and the Emir sent his cavalry to punish them. General Trézel boldly marched out with part of his garrison and effectually protected them. They then finally passed over to the French, and their mounted men formed a capital irregular cavalry, useful in every way. All this was due to General Trézel, as Count d'Erlon had ordered him to do nothing in case these wretched tribes were attacked.

Abd-el-Kader's orders on the subject of trading in cattle with the French, contrary to his wishes, were as follows: For the first offence, the unfortunate trader lost his right hand and right foot, and for the second offence his left hand and left foot,

THE CONQUEST OF ALGERIA

and for the third offence his head. As, however, all the punishments were carried out by the nearest butcher with the ordinary implements of his trade, it was found in practice that the second and third punishments never had to be inflicted, as all the culprits died from the effects of the first operation.

This interference of General Trézel led up to a fight with Abd-el-Kader, for the Emir took umbrage at being thus treated, and moved forwards towards the French general, who advanced to meet him on the 26th of June 1835 with 2,300 men, of whom 600 were cavalry. The Emir, for his part, had some 10,000 or 12,000 men, about 8,000 of whom were cavalry. He also had a battalion of foot drilled in European fashion by a German deserter from the Foreign Legion. This battalion was nearly 1,400 strong, and behaved very creditably.

Whilst speaking about Abd-el-Kader's regular soldiers, it may not be out of place to give the account of them, as written by Colonel Scott, somewhat later than this period, in his diary. He actually was with them, as he was serving under the orders of Abd-el-Kader against the French, though in a civilian capacity, or rather as military adviser on his staff. He was so much impressed with the fighting powers of the Arab regulars that he offered to assault Mostaganem (then held by the French) with these troops alone, and to be answerable with his life for the capture of the place.

He says that Abd-el-Kader's regular infantry amounted to seven battalions of from 1,200 to 1,300 each, and to each of these battalions was added a company of European deserters from the French service. These companies varied in strength, but some of them amounted to as many as 200 Europeans. This statement accounts for the fact that, at many of the actions in which the regular battalions of Abd-el-Kader were engaged, the French officers were astounded by the volleys of low abuse in the French tongue which came from the enemy's ranks. The infantry wore Turkish trousers, with a blue cloth jacket and a waist-belt. There was only one officer per company; the remainder of the work of commanding was carried out by the non-commissioned officers. The latter wore a silver plate on the uniform to distinguish them, whilst the single officer of the company wore two silver plates. The commanding officer of each regular infantry battalion was clad in a red uniform, and instead of being decorated with silver plates, wore three stripes on the cuff, which stripes were either of silver or gold braid, according to taste. The Emir also had regular cavalry, who were of good, hard-fighting material. His own particular mounted body-guard was clothed in red uniforms.

The battle-field was a wooded rough ground near the west bank of the Sig river. The engagement was begun in this place, by an attack by Arab skirmishers, on the French column's head and flanks. Three Polish companies of the Foreign Legion were sent to clear these skirmishers away, but were received with a volley by the regular battalion with the Arabs, which battalion had been cleverly concealed behind a ridge. The Poles were driven back in disorder. The Chasseurs d'Afrique promptly charged, but with no good results. Their colonel was killed in this charge. Some one gave a trumpeter the order to

THE CONQUEST OF ALGERIA

sound the retreat, and all then became confusion. General Trézel now showed them his soldierly qualities. Having lost an eye in the desperate fighting which marked the battle of Ligny in 1815, two days before the battle of Waterloo, a skirmish of this sort did not alarm him. Gathering up the battalion of African Light Infantry, who, it will be remembered, were the defaulters of the whole of the French Army, he sent them at the enemy, assisted by an Italian battalion of the Foreign Legion, backing them up with a line battalion. This was too much for the Arab regulars, who gave way, with the loss of their two senior officers. Then burning some wagons which had broken down during the momentary panic in the convoy, and any baggage that he had to remove to make room for the wounded, General Trézel slowly retired, and took up his bivouac for the night at a more open spot.

After remaining in bivouac over the 27th of June, the French fell back deliberately upon the port of Arzeu, for the purpose of sending their wounded by sea to Oran and of receiving a convoy of provisions and ammunition from the same place. The Arabs followed, engaging them warmly, and as the French approached some hills through which they had to pass they found that Abd-el-Kader had already seized them, unknown to the French, by the clever manœuvre of marching round the French, 1,500 cavalry, each with an infantryman mounted on the horse behind him. These lay in ambuscade, and when discovered successively defeated several attempts of the French advanced guard, consisting of the Italian battalion, to turn them out. This battalion then was seized with a panic, and rushed towards the rear. The Arabs ran in and commenced to loot the convoy.

Again General Trézel rallied the troops, but whilst he cleared the way in front, the cowardly drivers of the wagons containing the wounded, in their terror, drove into a morass which bordered the road, and, finding that their wagons were sticking, cut the traces and left their charges to their fate. Only one wagon-load of wounded was saved and one other wagon of the convoy. Arzeu was gained that night. The total French loss was 260 killed, and 17 prisoners, whilst 300 wounded were able to take themselves into Arzeu, and so were saved. At Arzeu General Trézel received orders from the Count d'Erlon to avoid any further engagements; and also the Count expressed his displeasure at the course the General had pursued in embroiling himself with Abd-el-Kader to save the Douair and Sméla tribes from massacre. However, most right-minded people will agree that General Trézel adopted the only possible line of conduct for a brave and honourable man to follow.

His troops were badly shaken by this check, but he was still full of energy. As he was not permitted to move out again to attack the enemy, he sent his wounded and infantry away by sea, and marched with the Chasseurs d'Afrique and the faithful Arabs of the Douair and Sméla tribes to Oran. This fight was always known by the French as the disaster of the Macta.

As an example of what General Trézel had to face it may be mentioned that the colonel of the Chasseurs d'Afrique was dismayed at the idea of this

THE CONQUEST OF ALGERIA

march, and strongly opposed it. This probably gives the key to much of the cause of this disaster, for the senior officers were too old, and preferred a peaceable life, with their pensions in view, to battling with a set of hard-fighting, blood-thirsty barbarians.

General Trézel was relieved of his command at Oran by order of the Count d'Erlon, and he sailed for France, respected by all, even the enemy, whilst d'Erlon was himself recalled on the 8th of July 1835, and his place was filled by the return of Marshal Clauzel.

The Count d'Erlon had not distinguished himself in his command. Anything favourable to the French, that had taken place, had occurred in spite of him.

One incident will show what extraordinary things were carried out by his orders. Whilst General Trézel was fighting for his life on the 26th and 28th of June 1835, a French brig of war captured a vessel delivering powder and 200 muskets to Abd-el-Kader, and on inquiry it was found that these had been sent secretly to him by the Count d'Erlon. Of course they were not treacherously sent to him, but the Count was so impressed with the necessity of keeping on friendly terms with him that he hoped by presents and flattery to convert him into a sincere friend of the French; and for this he was willing to sacrifice the wretched tribesmen who begged his protection. Naturally he did not know how events were shaping at Oran, or he would not have sent this powder, &c., for it must be remembered that this all occurred before the days of telegraphs, and that news travelled slowly in those times.

CHAPTER XII

THE Duc d'Orleans had arrived in Algiers to take part in the fighting. He was heir to the French throne, and naturally the fact of his being there, as well as the intense interest taken by the whole nation in repairing the check received by General Trézel, made the occupation of the country much more popular, than it before had been, in France.

It was determined once for all to break the power of Abd-el-Kader, and four line regiments were ordered from France to Oran. Their departure had, however, to be delayed on account of an outbreak of cholera in France, and also in Algeria. Whilst awaiting their arrival, Marshal Clauzel sent an expedition from Algiers to punish some neighbouring Arab tribe; 5,000 men were sent out, and after some fighting the enemy was dispersed with loss. Next day he was not to be seen, and his territory was ravaged from end to end, all his huts burnt, and his crops destroyed, and the column returned in triumph to Algiers only to find that the enemy, ascertaining that the column was too strong for him, had wisely absconded from his own territory, and had profitably spent the time of his enforced absence, in looting and murdering the French colonists on the farms near Algiers.

What these raids by Arabs meant to the

THE CONQUEST OF ALGERIA 103

poor French colonists is perhaps best shown by giving two instances, as taken from Colonel Scott's diary. He mentions that some Arabs went to a respectable settler's home near Algiers by night. They found the father was away on business, and only women in the house. A young servant girl came out, and seeing them, attempted to give the alarm, whereupon one of these ruffians cut off her head. The mother of the family, coming out to see what had occurred, was set upon with swords by the party and done to death. After looting the house the Arabs carried off the three little daughters, whose ages ranged from three years old up to nine years. When Colonel Scott came across the family, only the youngest girl was left alive, the remainder having died. He was instrumental in obtaining the poor child's release.

The other case was, if possible, more brutal, for he found that two French deserters living with the Arabs had gone down to a farm near a well-known building called Maison Carée, and had there found only two young girls, the daughters of the proprietor, who was absent. What evil treatment they subjected these unfortunate females to is not stated, but they returned to Abd-el-Kader's territory carrying the heads of their two poor victims. When such things were constantly occurring, it was little wonder if now and then the French soldiers paid back the enemy in their own coin.

As the troops began to pour into Oran, Marshal Clauzel had a fort constructed some ten miles out, at a place called Le Figuier, capable of holding 500 men. It could now be seen what his object was—Mascara, Abd-el-Kader's capital—and this was the first stage on the journey. On the 21st of November

1835 the Marshal and the Duc d'Orleans arrived from Algiers, and the Marshal promptly went to work to organise his expedition. Attributing the disaster of General Trézel to his great convoy, he did away with all wagons and carts and hired 700 camels from the friendly Arabs. As they did not come in so quickly as they were required, he surrounded the Arabs' tents one night and took the camels home with him. He then organised his force into four brigades. It consisted of some 11,000 men, of whom 10,000 were Europeans. The 26th of November 1835 this force was assembled at the fort of Le Figuier. Curiously enough, Abd-el-Kader had been fairly peaceable up to now. He had found that after his fight with General Trézel his army had vanished, each going home with his spoil, and he was left alone with his regular battalion. Thus little had happened since that time.

On the 29th of November the troops marched over the place where the fighting at the disaster of Macta had begun. On the 30th another fort was constructed on the left bank of the River Sig—yet another step towards Mascara. On the 1st of December there was a skirmish in the hills with some 4,000 Arabs. On the 3rd of December, as mentioned by the Duc d'Orleans in his ' Memoirs,' 10,000 Arab cavalry attacked the French after crossing the Sig, but were beaten off. They retreated and seized a position guarded on one flank by a wood and on the other by a mountain, which thus formed a defile through which the French would have to pass. Again they were driven off at the first attack of the French.

That night Marshal Clauzel's army camped on the River Habra. They crossed by a pontoon bridge on the 4th of December, and moved as if they were going north-east towards Mostaganem, but, suddenly turning to the right, moved into a gorge which led through some twenty-five miles of mountain towards Mascara. The enemy, deceived by the movement towards the north-east, were only holding the gorge with a few men, who were easily driven off. On the 5th, despite all hard work, the convoy was only able to move forward seven miles in the twenty-four hours.

On the 6th of December Marshal Clauzel left two brigades with the convoy and pushed on with the two others to Mascara. He arrived at nightfall in heavy rain, and found it empty with the exception of the Jews. These poor creatures had suffered much from the Arabs before they retreated, and many had been massacred, and their bodies thrown into wells. The arsenal of Abd-el-Kader was taken here, including twenty-two cannon, and the howitzer equipage captured at Macta. After blowing up the citadel, and destroying the walls of the town, the French in Mascara retired to the other two brigades, which they joined on the 10th of December, having had heavy rain during the whole of four days. Short of provisions, the army arrived on the 12th of December at Mostaganem. The total losses in this expedition were 200 killed and wounded.

Marshal Clauzel about this time expressed his opinion on what was required to bring Algeria into thorough subjection to the French. It was a garrison at Mascara, Tlemcen, Oran, Mostaganem, and at Sig, in the province of Oran. In Algiers garrisons at Blida and Kolea, and at Medea and Miliana, with two connecting forts on the Col de Tenia, whilst in

Constantine he proposed to hold Bougie, Boné, La Calle, and Constantine itself, and in each of the three provinces to keep a column constantly moving about, 5,000 strong. He calculated that 40,000 men would be required for the first two years, and after that 20,000 with some native troops. His calculations were probably more or less correct, if the columns had been well used by their commanders.

In the meantime, after his return viâ Mostaganem to Oran he found as a result of his expedition to Mascara, that a large number of the two powerful tribes of Douair and Sméla, who had been with Abd-el-Kader, now returned back and joined their own tribes in alliance with the French, whilst he also heard that the Coulouglis in the citadel at Tlemcen were hard pressed by the Arabs who were blockading them. Abd-el-Kader moved back into the partially destroyed city of Mascara, and decided that it was not too bad for repair, and again established himself there. He at once carried out a vigorous raid against the Douair and Sméla, carrying off some of their cattle, and then, doubling hurriedly back, moved to Tlemcen, caught the Coulouglis napping, and killed sixty of them. The remainder held out bravely in the citadel.

On the 8th of January 1836 Marshal Clauzel marched out from Oran with a force consisting of three brigades counting in all some 7,000 men, including friendly Arabs. He arrived in Tlemcen on the 13th of January about midday, being met by the brave Coulouglis, who for six years had held their own against the Arab forces. They only numbered 700 men, of whom 450 only had firearms. The French occupied the town, Abd-el-Kader having moved away in the hopes

THE CONQUEST OF ALGERIA 107

that the French would shortly retire, as they had done at Mascara. Marshal Clauzel sent the friendly Arabs after him, supported by the 1st Brigade. These Arabs had a grudge against Abd-el-Kader, and pressed him hard. He escaped with difficulty, and a large number of his men were taken.

The Marshal then decided to try and find a short way from Tlemcen to the sea. The total distance to the island of Rachgoun, by the valley of the Tafna, was only 30 miles. By the way he had come it was 90 miles. On the 25th of January he tried to find his way through this valley. He found that the road was much too bad to take his army through. He fought an action on the 26th and 27th against the energetic Abd-el-Kader, who had strengthened himself by calling on the mountain tribes of Kabyles for support; and returned to Tlemcen on the 28th of January. Marshal Clauzel, adopting the customs of the empire, called for a contribution of £6,000 from Tlemcen, and ill-treated the inhabitants, including the gallant garrison, to try and squeeze the money out of them. Much harm was done to the French cause thereby, and the French Home Government was most justly indignant, and caused the money to be returned, but it was not easy to remove the bad impression caused by such base treatment of allies.

Leaving a garrison of 550 men in Tlemcen besides the Coulouglis, all under a captain of engineers, named Cavaignac, the column set out for Oran on the 7th of February, arriving at that town on the 12th of that month.

The Marshal returned to Algiers on the 19th of

February. Authorities differ as to the number of troops left with Cavaignac. The figures above given are those mentioned by M. Rousset, whilst Sir R. Lambert Playfair states that his garrison only numbered 275 men all told.

The 'Memoirs' of the Duc d'Orleans pays a fine and well-deserved tribute to the gallant garrison of Coulouglis, who for so long held the barracks of Meshouar against the tribes from Morocco and against Abd-el-Kader. He says: 'During six long years this brave garrison had fought all the time, deserted, ignored by the rest of the world, without hope of any help, without any place to retreat on, and with no possibility of a capitulation, fated to disappear in the middle of the Arabs who slaughter the vanquished; it resisted the enemy, the discouragements, and the privations. It had even resisted "l'aveugle complicité" of France with Abd-el-Kader. Having only 400 muskets for 800 men, it was obliged to search in the ranks of its enemies for the arms, which it required, in individual struggles, of which the singular character recalled the combats of antiquity.'

And yet these were the very men that Marshal Clauzel tried to obtain £6,000 from as a war contribution. Truly a strange reward for their gallant defence of the citadel, as much in the interests of the French as in defence of their own necks.

CHAPTER XIII

WITH a view of supporting the French Bey of Medea, whose subjects declined to have anything to do with him, Marshal Clauzel decided to march to that town. He therefore formed a column at Boufarik on the 30th of March 1836, of a total strength of 6,200 men. Of this force 1,200 were cavalry, and there were five companies of engineers, as he had determined to make the road to Medea passable for wheeled traffic. By the 5th of April the road was made to the top of the Pass of Mouzaia. A party had been dispatched to the town of Medea, and duly returned, having established a garrison of 600 Coulouglis, who were natives of the town, and having armed them with muskets. On the way back this party attacked an Arab tribe—one of those who had been most truculent—and duly destroyed their dwellings and captured their herds. By the 9th of April all the troops were back in their various camps round Algiers. They had suffered a loss of 300 in killed and wounded, as there had been constant fighting.

This small expedition finished, another one claims our notice at Oran: General d'Arlanges, who was in charge in the province of Oran, had been directed to move to the mouth of the Tafna, opposite to the island of Rachgoun, with a view of working up the

Tafna to Tlemcen, which it will be remembered was only thirty miles from the sea by this route. It was an idea of Marshal Clauzel, but the men for the expedition were not sufficiently numerous, and General d'Arlanges, though brave, was but a poor general. On the 7th of April, then, General d'Arlanges formed a column of 3,200 men and slowly moved to the mouth of the Tafna. Towards the end of his march, which lasted till the 16th of April, he was fiercely attacked not only by the Arabs but by the Kabyles, who appear to have been even hardier foes than the former. At the mouth of the Tafna he was blockaded, but he duly established a fortified camp, and then taking some 2,000 men, infantry and cavalry, with 8 guns, he moved up the Tafna on the 25th of April. So soon as he got into the broken ground he was assailed by numerous bands and by Abd-el-Kader himself, who tried to cut off the French retreat. The French general was wounded, and the column retired, fighting every step of the way. The Kabyles rushed upon the bayonets, seized the cannon with their hands, and altogether fought magnificently. The French regained their camp to find that it had been attacked in their absence, but that the attack had been beaten off. Their losses were 40 killed and 300 wounded.

Colonel Scott relates one anecdote of the battle of the Tafna, which shows Abd-el-Kader's staff in action, and their modes of courtesy to one another whilst so engaged.

He noticed one person of great importance with Abd-el-Kader, who always spoke through his nose, and even then spoke with difficulty. He was informed

THE CONQUEST OF ALGERIA

that this personage was the intendant-general of Abd-el-Kader, and at the combat of the Tafna, when the Emir's horse was shot under him, he was directed to dismount and give him his own horse. Being fifty-five years old, he was slow in dismounting, whereupon one of the Arab staff swung the butt of his gun round, and struck him on the nose, breaking it, and knocking all his front teeth down his throat. Apparently he bore no malice, for he continued to serve his master in 1841 when Colonel Scott met him.

The effect of this skirmish on the surrounding natives was bad, and many who had been inclined to support the French revolted. The French Government was equal to the occasion and promptly sent some 7,500 fresh troops from France under General Bugeaud. He decided to make many small columns, provided with pack animals, which could move quickly across the broken country after the enemy.

With various reinforcements brought round by sea he was able to take a column from the fort at the mouth of the Tafna to Oran, numbering some 6,000 men, of whom 400 only were cavalry, leaving a garrison in this fort of 1,200 men. The Arabs had been expecting him to make an attempt to move up the Tafna again, but finding out his plan, hurried to engage him, but only a skirmish ensued, and on the 17th of June he arrived at Oran. It is interesting for a soldier to see what this general said in his report on the campaigning, in this country, to his government. He wrote more or less as follows: 'Eighty mules per 1,000 men can carry ten days' supplies for those men, four days' provisions can be carried by those men themselves, fourteen days is quite long enough for an expedition to last in this country.' He added that the officers should be young and energetic—which last is a point that all nations are prone to forget. On the 19th of June, General Bugeaud moved out with the same column strengthened by some 800 more cavalry, with large supplies for Tlemcen. On the 24th of June, Abd-el-Kader attacked him with all his forces. The Chasseurs d'Afrique, boldly led, charged his cavalry in front, whilst the Sméla and Douair warriors as gallantly charged the enemy's flank. After a stiff combat the Emir's forces fled in disorder and the column pursued its way. The garrison at Tlemcen was found to be in a very flourishing state under command of Captain Cavaignac. The surrounding country had been ruined by the policy of the Arabs, who had sent 120,000 head of cattle to graze in the vicinity, thus eating up grass and crops indiscriminately. A curious letter from one of the colonels during this march shows that the French infantry was not of the same composition throughout. He mentions the column as in part consisting of 'conscripts commanded by whimperers'; he adds that most of the men could not march twelve or fifteen miles. General Bugeaud mentions the same thing as to their marching powers, and states that one regiment was thoroughly demoralised. He further says that four men of this regiment committed suicide in a march of some twelve miles. He again repeats that he considers it the fault of the officers, and recommends that picked ones be selected, first to command regiments, then columns. General

Bugeaud then returned from Tlemcen and headed for the valley of the Tafna, from which Marshal Clauzel had been obliged to retire. Instead of entering it he turned it by the right, and after reconnoitring it and finding that it was practically unforceable against even a small army, he pushed on, by the road he had taken, to the camp on the Tafna, which he reached on the 29th of June. He organised a second convoy and led it again up towards the Tafna gorge, and then camped for the night, but at midnight he stole away from his bivouac, and, by the same path he had before taken, found his way towards Tlemcen, over a ridge 1,600 feet high. On the 6th of July the Arabs attempted to attack the convoy in the rear guard, whilst another party should hold up the advanced guard. Their numbers were 3,000 horsemen, and 3,000 Kabyle foot. The Chasseurs d'Afrique boldly charged the Arab horsemen, but had to retire on account of the hot fire on their flank from the Kabyle infantry. The Chasseurs rallied under the fire of the mountain battery, and charged again, and drove the Arabs from the field. Then the Kabyle infantry was savagely attacked, but Abd-el-Kader moved up with an infantry regiment some 1,500 strong to their support. After some hard fighting all the Kabyles and the Arab regulars were driven from the field. The convoy had meanwhile been parked in square, and so soon as the main fighting was over, moved placidly forward towards Tlemcen. The French lost, in this well-conducted fight, only 32 killed and 70 wounded. The Arabs lost very heavily; 130 of the Emir's regulars were saved from the slaughter by General Bugeaud himself, who dashed upon their captors (his friendly Arabs), and, with blows of the flat of his sword, made them cease killing these unfortunates. He paid a ransom for them to their captors according to custom. Over 700 muskets alone were taken, besides half a dozen flags. The General went to Tlemcen on the following day, and sent out a flying column to reap crops and to collect grain on the beaten tribes' ground.

Owing to the way in which the Arab tribes stored their grain it was most easy, with the assistance of a renegade Arab, to find the whole of the corn of a tribe. The method adopted by the natives was as follows: forty or fifty pits were made, each capable of holding 1,000 bushels of grain, and a sandy and dry soil was selected. The sides of these pits were plastered with mortar all over to a thickness of one inch. The mouths of these pits would be only large enough for a man to get into them, and would be some three feet below the surface. The pits having been filled with grain, their mouths were then plastered over and covered with soil to the level of the ground. The soil excavated from the pits was then carried away, so as not to betray the fact of their existence. The grass soon grew over the disturbed soil, and the grain in the pits, or silos, as they were called, remained good for twenty or thirty years. The French used to employ Arabs, who had quarrelled with their tribes, to show them where the silos were, and thus could destroy the whole food-supply of a tribe in a very short time.

On the 12th of July the French moved slowly back to Oran, which place they reached on the 19th, having destroyed the crops of the enemy the whole way home. This most happy little campaign restored the French prestige, and General Bugeaud was created a lieut.-general and returned to France immediately.

CHAPTER XIV

MARSHAL CLAUZEL had at length obtained permission from the French Government to make an expedition to capture Constantine. He determined to make Boné his starting point, and to reduce the distance from the French base to Constantine (which is some 70 miles as the crow flies, but much more of course by road) it was decided to erect fortified camps on the road. The first one was made some 15 miles out and was named Fort Clauzel. A reconnaissance was also made to Guelma some 50 miles on the road to Constantine, but so far, Boné could not spare enough troops to form a garrison for this place.

The troops for the expedition, however, commenced to assemble at Boné, and all were more or less collected by the 31st of October 1836. They numbered some 8,000 men, and within the first week 2,000 of them were in hospital with fever. These troops, be it understood, were seasoned men, all being got from Algeria: as no reinforcements were sent from France, Oran, Algiers, and Bougie all furnished what troops they could spare. The Marshal himself arrived on the 31st of October, and the Duc de Nemours, son of the King of France, also came to take part in the expedition. For these operations the engineers, artillery, and army train demanded 1,500 mules. All that were at first procurable was some 500. So the expedition

THE CONQUEST OF ALGERIA 117

was delayed until the 8th of November, when the advanced guard, 2,700 strong, moved off to Guelma.

Reinforcements having arrived, the remainder of the army, now numbering with the advanced guard about 9,000 men, marched on the 13th of November. The men each carried seven days' food on the person, and must have been very heavily weighted. The weak point of the expedition, however, was that no siege guns were taken, as there were no means of conveying them. Six field guns and ten mountain guns comprised the whole of the artillery. On the 15th of November the French column abandoned their engineers' wagons, including the escalading ladders, also much of the corn for the horses, as the road was impracticable for vehicles. Leaving 150 infantry as a guard at Guelma, and leaving also some 100 sick and 150,000 cartridges, the army pressed on during the 16th in two columns, one on either side of the River Seybouse, camping at Mjez Ahmar. The 18th of November the army crossed a high neck called Ras el Akba, and bivouacked on the side near Constantine. On the 19th of November it camped at Oued Zenati. The road was very sandy now, and wood being scarce, each infantryman had a bunch of firewood tied above his knapsack, and carried a piece as a walking stick, with a view to cooking his rations until their arrival at the city of Constantine.

From the 19th the weather broke. First storms of rain came on, and they were followed by heavy hail, and this continued during the 20th and the 21st of November. Twenty men were frozen to death on the night of the 20th. On the 22nd the French found that the small streams had become impassable on account of the rain. As the weather was so awful the Marshal did not feel justified in waiting for them to go down, so he sent some swimmers across and stretched ropes from bank to bank, held by groups of men at either end. So soon as the Marshal had crossed, he pushed on with a mounted escort, expecting to find the city deserted. It was, however, strongly held, and the garrison appeared determined to make a vigorous resistance.

Constantine is built on a rocky plateau, which is surrounded on three sides by a ravine; which ravine is stated to be 1,000 feet deep. At the bottom of the chasm flows a stream called the Roummel, and the breadth of this gorge varies from 200 feet to 400 feet. When Marshal Clauzel and the French Army approached the town, the Roummel was in flood, and his skirmishers, who wished to establish themselves on the fourth side, on which side the town was approachable, found that they had to ford the river with the water up to their shoulders, and that the current was running so swiftly that they had to link hands and help each other across. Later on, when the Marshal wished to send a message across to order the assault to take place, it was necessary to send it by the hand of a swimmer.

Across this ravine at the north-eastern angle of the city, at the time of the French expedition, stood a wonderful bridge. It had been erected by the Romans, and was called El Kantara by their Arab successors. Taking advantage of the fact that four natural rock arches spanned the stream of the Roummel, at some 200 feet above it, these great

THE CONQUEST OF ALGERIA 119

builders erected on top of Nature's bridge, one of their own. Even then the height was too great for a single arch, so the bridge ran on two series of arches, one below the other. The actual height of the Roman work was 220 feet from the top of the road to the foundations, and from the foundations again down to the surface of the water in the stream at normal times was 184 feet. This mavellous structure is now in ruins. Sir R. Lambert Playfair states that suddenly without warning the foundations gave way in 1857, and it then became unsafe, and was battered down by some heavy guns by the French troops; it had last been repaired in 1793 by the Turks. A modern iron bridge now spans the ravine. The enemy's side of the bridge of El Kantara was well guarded by gates, and there was also a tunnel or covered path on their side leading down to the water below, so that the inhabitants could freely descend for water without danger. The usual side from which Constantine was besieged was the fourth side. It had three gates on this front called respectively Bab-el-Djidid, Bab-el-Raiba, and Bab-el-Djabia. Here the town walls could be approached and regular trenches could have been made. Unfortunately for the French, however, they had no siege material with them.

Constantine, of which the population is some 50,000 souls, had been besieged before. In fact it had a historical record of 160 sieges, and its known history commenced before B.C. 230, when the town was called Cirta, and was in alliance with Carthage. Hannibal's sister was married at that time to the king of the country named Narva, and they both resided at Cirta. It changed its name to Constantine in A.D. 313, after being captured by the Romans, and now in A.D. 1836 it was again going through the experience of another siege, but this time an unsuccessful one.

The French Army followed Marshal Clauzel and came up to him whilst he was still studying the city and looking down into the ravine, of which it was impossible to see the bottom on that day. He determined to make two attacks: one on the bridge of El Kantara, the other on the sort of isthmus which led up to the city on the fourth side. To get to the latter, as noted before, it was necessary to cross the Roummel, and the enemy trooped down to oppose this crossing, but were driven back by the fire of the skirmishers, and when the French did cross, the Turks fled in wild panic to the city. Many thought that it would have been wise to enter with the flying enemy, others said that if this had been done no Frenchman would have returned alive.

Probably if sufficient numbers had entered, the city would have been taken. The opportunity passed, however, and did not return.

The guns of the place opened upon the French as they advanced, and then it was more plainly seen that the Bey of Constantine meant to fight for his beylik. As the night fell a snowstorm came on, but the French took up their positions round the town, chased a few lingering skirmishers into it, and threw a few shells and rockets into the place. At daybreak next morning, the 23rd of November, the enemy made a sortie. The attacked troops, with their muskets wet with the snow, were unable to reply to the attack, excepting with the bayonet. Fortunately the 2nd Light Infantry had slept in a building called the Bardo, and rushing out, with dry arms, took the enemy in flank and drove them back. A curious incident occurred whilst the troops were taking up their positions. Some wagons laden with spirits having stuck in the mud, the escort belonging to the 62nd Regiment of the Line determined to take away the horses and burn the wagons, but they first helped themselves liberally to the spirits and became incapable of moving, and in this state were caught by the Arabs, who killed 116 of the drunkards. The garrison of the town consisted first of Turks—these men had been recruited from Constantinople and from Smyrna, &c. Besides these, the townsmen were armed, and a strong contingent of Kabyles had come into the town to help, as the defence had been confided by the Bey to a Kabyle named Ben Aissa, whilst the Bey himself traversed the country raising all the tribes against the French.

During the 23rd a cannonade went on between the fortress guns and the French field guns. At night, the gates were examined, under a heavy fire, by a small party of French, but were found more or less intact, though pierced by cannon balls. They found the besieged on the alert, and several of the examining party were slain by their fire.

On the 25th of November the last rations were issued to the men. The rations consisted of rice and brandy. None had been issued for three days before this. The enemy made a sortie from the gates and the Arabs attacked from the rear; these last were only beaten off after hard fighting. The Marshal determined to attack at midnight on the 25th–26th of November, and to blow in two gates with powder bags. The gates chosen for attack were those of El Kantara and Bab-el-Raiba.

The moon shone brightly at midnight. A heavy fire swept away the assailants, and they were beaten back with heavy loss in both cases. The only course open to the French, under these circumstances, was to retreat towards Boné. At three o'clock in the morning the greater part of the wounded were sent away, many on the horses of the Chasseurs d'Afrique, others were carried by their comrades in blankets. The orders were, that all should be on the move by five o'clock, marching on the road by which they had advanced, and that a battalion, from one of the camps on the way, should be brought up to assist them. Unfortunately it took longer to move than had been expected, and the rear guard, composed of the 2nd Light Infantry, less than 300 strong, had to move off, in full daylight, under a heavy cannonade from the city, and fiercely attacked by the Kabyles. As they were retiring, they found a post of African Light Infantry which had been forgotten in the confusion, and of which half had been killed before they were rescued. Some of the unfortunate wounded were drowned in crossing the streams during the retirement. The 2nd Light Infantry was promptly surrounded by the Arab horsemen. It formed square, and, waiting till the cavalry had closed on it to within forty yards, opened a rolling fire which in two minutes drove off the Arabs, after covering the plain with killed and wounded men and horses. Out of the 300 men of the 2nd Light Infantry, seventeen were

THE CONQUEST OF ALGERIA 123

killed and forty wounded. Still the square held steadily on and covered the retreat of the army. The name of the major commanding it was 'de Changarnier.' He was an excellent soldier and very proud of his regiment. Just before the charge of Arab cavalry on his square, which has been recorded above, he addressed his men somewhat as follows: 'I see that there are some 6,000 mounted Arabs attacking us. We are 300. It is an even chance; 300 of us are as good as 6,000 of them.'

The column only retreated twelve miles that day, but the troops had now been got into hand and the Arabs, though very numerous, dared not push home their attacks. The Duc d'Orleans in his 'Memoirs' notes that the women of the town poured out and killed the French wounded with every barbarity and insult which they could devise, whilst the townsmen followed and attacked the rear guard. A certain number of wounded were left behind. Some had been sheltered in caves and could not be got out in time, and many had no means of conveyance. Everything was done that could be done, but the men were so weak from overwork and want of food, that they could hardly carry themselves, much less their wounded comrades. Marshal Clauzel's great anxiety in his retreat was, lest his men should be 'rushed' by the Kabyles in the mountain passes and be overthrown in hand-to-hand combat, so that, throughout the retreat, musketry fire was opened at long ranges to keep the enemy at a distance. The French left behind them in their retirement from Constantine twenty-five baggage wagons and all their medical stores, many muskets and two howitzers.

A curious incident is mentioned of the first day's march. Two wagons were abandoned, there being no horses to drag them. Twenty footsore men mounted these wagons, apparently under the belief that horses would be obtained from somewhere, and that they would be driven away. Despite repeated orders they refused to descend; the army moved on, and they were left behind, and within five minutes every one of them was butchered. The column struggled on, being less pressed as they left Constantine further behind them. At Guelma they received food, and the column finally entered Boné on the 1st of December.

The losses of this expedition were surprisingly small. Some 500 killed and some 300 wounded are reported by some authorities as being beyond the mark, but it is probable that the numbers more nearly approached 1,000. There was much sickness in the ranks afterwards and many deaths. Reinforcements were promptly sent from France. The Tirailleurs d'Afrique were formed of volunteers from all regiments in France, and the Foreign Legion, which had been temporarily lent to Spain, sent back a battalion, &c. On the 30th of January 1837, to add to the troubles of the French, the powder magazine of the citadel at Boné blew up, killing and wounding some 300 soldiers. Guelma was garrisoned with 1,000 men under Colonel Duvivier, which portended a second advance on Constantine in the near future. Marshal Clauzel left Algeria in January 1837, and was shortly after removed from the office of governor-general.

CHAPTER XV

A STRANGE peculiarity of the campaign in Algeria has to be noticed. It was, that almost all the generals were what we should call 'Members of Parliament,' and that according to their votes so, as a rule, they received employment in Algeria. Marshal Clauzel was a member of the Chamber of Deputies, and so was General Bugeaud; so also was the A.D.C. of Marshal Clauzel. Therefore, when General Bugeaud opposed the French Government's views on Algeria, they not unnaturally did not select that excellent soldier to succeed Marshal Clauzel, but chose a General de Damremont, who was more in accord with their views. But knowing what a good general Bugeaud was, they sent him to Oran in a semi-independent position, whilst Damremont, appointed as governor-general, made arrangements for the renewal of the attack on Constantine.

This sort of political soldier or sailor has been known in England, though not prominently for many years. In the time of our great wars with France at least from 1776 to 1800 the admirals almost always were in Parliament, and were appointed to command or not, according as their Government was able to make political capital out of them or not. Readers may remember the courteous way in which Admiral Howe, of glorious First of June fame, was always scrupulously addressed as 'Mr.' Howe in the House of Commons. In many ways the fact that politics should be mixed up with commands is unpleasant, and fortunately it seldom now occurs.

Before General Bugeaud arrived at Oran a most interesting swindle had taken place. It will be remembered that 130 of Abd-el-Kader's regulars had been taken prisoners in one action. The Emir much desired the return of these men. The garrison at Tlemcen required a new convoy. A clever Moorish merchant persuaded the French Government to hand over the prisoners to Abd-el-Kader as an act of clemency. He also offered to put a convoy into Tlemcen without troubling the military to escort it. He was, of course, to be well paid by the French for this. Still pursuing his knavish courses, he then told the Emir that if he would revictual Tlemcen at his own cost, this would be taken as an equivalent, and the prisoners would be at once set free. All this was promptly carried out, and the merchant made a most satisfactory increase in his banking account.

Both Generals Bugeaud and de Damremont disembarked, at Oran and Algiers respectively, about the 1st of April 1837. The number of troops in Algeria had been raised by reinforcements from France from 31,000 to 43,000.

On the 17th of May the French moved out of Oran, revictualled Tlemcen, and then marched back to the camp on the Tafna without seeing an enemy. The march is noticeable because they used pack transport entirely, viz. 550 mules and 300 camels; but the mules were dreadfully knocked about by their

THE CONQUEST OF ALGERIA 127

bad pack-saddles. The column demolished the camp of the Tafna and removed the garrison. In the meantime some sort of a treaty was patched up by General Bugeaud and Abd-el-Kader. It was known as the Treaty of the Tafna, and its principal conditions were that the Emir should recognise French authority, and that they should make over to him a large part of the interior of the provinces of Oran and Algiers, including the town of Tlemcen. After long hesitation, this treaty was accepted by the French Government; but it was not a satisfactory one. The French general met the Emir at a conference, when 10,000 beautifully mounted Arab horsemen surrounded this extraordinary man, half saint and half warrior. Tlemcen was abandoned, and the Coulouglis were permitted to withdraw if they did not make peace with Abd-el-Kader. Most of them retired to Oran, where many joined the Zouaves.

Some small fighting took place on the 25th of May with some Kabyles, who opposed the erection of a fort some miles to the south-east of Algiers. The natives numbered some thousands, but were defeated, leaving 100 dead on the field, whilst the French lost 70 killed and wounded.

The French Government, pleased to have made a treaty with Abd-el-Kader, decided to try and come to some arrangement with the Bey of Constantine. He, however, would not listen to any moderate terms, so the arrangements for a second expedition to Constantine were pushed on apace. The Duc d'Orleans and his brother, the Duc de Nemours, were both anxious to accompany the expedition. The Duc de Nemours was sent. General Valée, an able Artillery general, was also sent to command the artillery, and General Fleury to command the engineers.

A fortified camp was erected at Mjez Ahmar, on the road to Constantine. On the 12th of September 1837 a small force of 2,500 troops carried out a reconnaissance towards Constantine, with the governor-general in command. No fighting of importance took place, but the troops noticed the extraordinary difference between the northern and southern slopes of the hills they crossed, the latter being a sort of desert, the other fruitful. This column returned on the 13th of September, leaving out some 1,200 men to improve the roads for the further advance of the troops.

On the 22nd of September, the governor having returned to Boné to meet the Duc de Nemours, the enemy seized the opportunity to attack the camp of Mjez Ahmar. They numbered some 7,500 men, and attacked for two days in very good style, but were beaten off with heavy loss. The French lost some 70 killed and wounded.

Despite the cholera having broken out in a regiment sent from France, and the fact that some 2,500 men were in hospital, principally with fever, the preparations for the expedition steadily went forward, and by the 1st of October 1837 the army was ready to move off from Guelma in two columns. The 1st Division marched a day in advance, and escorted the siege train; the 2nd, following behind, brought the convoy with it. It is interesting to go into details of this important expedition. The strength of the infantry amounted to 7,000, whilst the cavalry were 1,500 strong. The artillery numbered 1,200, and the engineers some 1,000 men. This time siege guns were taken, besides the field guns. The siege train consisted of four 24-pounders, four 16-pounders, two 8-inch howitzers, four 6-inch howitzers, and three 8-inch mortars. Half a million cartridges for the infantry were also taken. Two thousand five hundred mules and horses were in the convoy, and fourteen days' provisions were carried by the commissariat, whilst the men carried eight days' rations on the person. The infantry were so overburdened by this weight that less needful things were left behind, and beyond their muskets, bayonets, and cartridge pouch, little else was carried by the men, excepting the eight days' provisions and a portion of a *tente d'abre*. Four brigades made up the two divisions, and the troops employed were as follows:—

First Brigade—Commander, Duc de Nemours: One battalion of Zouaves; one battalion of the 2nd Light Infantry; two battalions of the 17th Light Infantry; six squadrons of the 3rd Chasseurs d'Afrique; two mountain and two field guns.

Second Brigade—Commander, General Trézel: Two battalions of the 23rd Regiment; a Turkish battalion; the Tirailleurs d'Afrique; the unattached company of Bougie; Native Irregular Cavalry; two field and two mountain guns.

Third Brigade—Commander, General Rullière: One battalion of Regiment d'Afrique; one battalion of the Foreign Legion; one battalion of the 26th Regiment; two squadrons of the 1st Chasseurs d'Afrique; two squadrons of Regular Native Cavalry; four mountain guns.

Fourth Brigade—Commander, Colonel Combe:

One battalion of the 26th Regiment; two battalions of the 47th Regiment; two field and two mountain guns.

Total strength, 10,700 fighting men.

Without adventure, but after some bad weather, the whole French Army reached Constantine by noon of the 6th of October 1837. The inhabitants shrieked curses on the army from the walls. Some guns opened on the French. Red flags were hoisted on many buildings, and some 300 Kabyles made a sortie, but were easily driven back by the Zouaves, assisted by the 2nd Light Infantry. Constantine looked much the same, only one of the gates which had been attacked, called El Kantara, had been walled up, and a new gate opened, in a spot covered from artillery fire. All the houses outside the walls had been removed, and all the tops of the walls of the town had been crenated; also those houses which overlooked the walls had been loopholed. The Bey of Constantine had withdrawn again into the country to raise the Arab tribes, whilst Ben Aissa, the Kabyle, again was governor of the town, and, besides the same garrison as last year, had brought in some 500 gunners from Asia Minor, supposed to be experts. On the night of the 6th of October working parties were sent out to make approaches and batteries. On the 7th the enemy made a sortie with 1,000 Turks and Kabyles, whilst some 3,000 Arab cavalry attacked the French from the rear. They were all driven off after hard fighting. Heavy rain then came on, and interfered greatly during the night with the arming of the batteries. In one case, in particular, all the armament intended for one siege battery found its way in the darkness to the bottom of a neighbouring

THE CONQUEST OF ALGERIA 131

ravine. It consisted of one 24-pounder and two 16-pounders. It is not necessary to go into the details of the attack: it is sufficient to say that the main attack was naturally made on the side which could be reached without crossing the ravines, whilst other batteries were erected to sweep the ramparts guarding this side, to crush the fire of the citadel, and to bombard the city. The chief difficulties were, to level the platforms of the batteries, which were built on ledges of rock, and to form parapets for the batteries and for the parallels. Stones formed into a wall did for this last; but sandbags were used for the second purposes, and, owing to the scarcity of earth, had to be filled where earth could be found and then passed from hand to hand by a chain of infantrymen, whilst the heavy rain washed the earth out of the bags so fast, that very often they were more than half empty on arrival at the battery. The rain still continued, but the batteries opened fire on the morning of the 9th of October 1837, at seven o'clock. By one o'clock the fire of the place was crushed, but on the whole little other result appeared.

On the 10th of October a very serious sortie was made by the besieged, but they were again repulsed after a hard struggle. The rain at length ceased, and the works were pushed forward. The batteries on the 11th began to open a breach in the wall near the gate known as El Raiba, but the masonry of the wall was very firm, and for a long time resisted all the efforts of the French gunners.

General de Damremont now summoned the town, sending the message by a young Turkish soldier, who was drawn up by the garrison into the town by a rope let down over the walls. The summons promised safety to all, and that they should be left in undisturbed possession of their houses and goods. The messenger did not return until next morning, and it was feared that he had been slain; but next day he was sent back unhurt, with the message that if the Christians wanted food, the Turks were quite willing to share theirs with them, but that they (the French) would never enter Constantine so long as one of the garrison lived. On the night of the 11th–12th of October a breaching battery was made within 130 yards of the wall, and armed with four cannon. At eight o'clock that morning the governor-general was killed by a discharge from the walls. He had just been warned that he was standing in a dangerous place, but, occupied in examining the ground and the breach, he only replied, 'It is all the same,' and immediately fell dead.

The Duc d'Orleans in his 'Memoirs' mentions that General de Damremont insisted on wearing his white-plumed hat whilst making the reconnaissance, and this made him so noticeable that he was specially singled out by all the enemy's marksmen, and so lost his life. His chief of the staff, General Perregaux, hastened to raise him up, and was at once shot through the head. General Damremont was greatly respected by his men, a sure sign that he was a brave man and just. General Valée, the general commanding the artillery, now took command of the siege as being the senior present. He really had been senior

THE CONQUEST OF ALGERIA

to the late commander, but had willingly served under him.

The breaching battery opened fire at one o'clock on the 12th of October. It was supplied with ammunition by infantrymen running across the open some 300 yards, under a heavy fire, carrying the ammunition in their arms, and their losses in this unusual duty were surprisingly small. During the afternoon a demand for a twenty-four hours' truce had been made by the besieged, but the French refused to treat unless the gates of the town were first given up to them.

By six o'clock the wall was shattered, and the earth inside had poured out and formed a sort of roadway over the breach.

Again referring to the 'Memoirs' of the Duc d'Orleans, we find that one of the breaches was over thirty-three feet in width, and that they were thoroughly reconnoitred previous to the advance of the storming columns. Two captains who volunteered for this perilous duty were both wounded whilst examining this particular breach, but both were able to return to make their report. Three storming columns were now told off. The first numbered some 550 men, composed of those good soldiers the Zouaves, and the 2nd Light Infantry, with some sappers. The second party numbered nearly 700 men, and the third column the same number. Both these last were picked from various corps.

The Duc d'Orleans gives slightly different particulars, which are here quoted for comparison.

The number of columns he gives as three, and then gives their composition, as follows :—

First Column — Commanded by Lieut.-Colonel de Lamoricière (wounded in the assault).
Major Vieux, Engineers (killed in the assault).
Eighty sappers, under Captain Hachet (killed in the assault).
300 Zouaves, under Captain Sansay (killed in the assault).
Two companies of the 2nd Light Infantry, under Major Serigny (killed in the assault).
Second Column—Commanded by Colonel Combe (killed in the assault).
Captain Potier, Engineers (killed in the assault).
Forty sappers, under Captain Guignard (killed in the assault).
300 of the 17th Light Infantry, under Major Leclere.
100 of the 3rd Battalion d'Afrique.
100 of the Foreign Legion.
Third Column—Commanded by Colonel Corbin.
Detachment of the 17th Light Infantry.
        "   Tirailleurs d'Afrique.
        "   23rd Regiment of the Line.
        "   26th Regiment of the Line.

And he further states that the grand total of the three assaulting columns was 1,600, which are somewhat smaller numbers than those given by M. Rousset.

A fire was kept up on the breach during the night of the 12th-13th of October. General Valée then warned the officers of the storming columns that if the town was not carried by ten o'clock on the 13th of October the army would have to retreat at that hour. At daybreak the artillery opened with round shot on

THE CONQUEST OF ALGERIA 135

the breach to sweep away some repairs that the besieged had done to the summit, which repairs consisted of bags, presumably filled with earth, and of pieces of wood. These destroyed, the guns opened with grape, and the columns rushed to the assault at seven o'clock.

The Duc d'Orleans states that at the time of the assault only five cannon balls remained with the French. These were fired at 7 a.m., and under the cloud of smoke and dust raised by the discharge the storming parties rushed for the breach, with a shout from the French soldiers of 'En-foncée Mahomet; Jesus Christ prend la semaine.' A very free translation of this phrase may be taken as: 'Down with (or bury) Mahomet; Jesus Christ is orderly officer this week.'

The columns mounted the breach, and then they should, as arranged, have divided, some going to the right, others to the left, whilst others went straight forward; but it was not easy to turn to the right or left on account of the débris, and all the time a hail of bullets came from the loopholed houses before referred to. Still the French pressed on, and first gained a footing by storming the barracks of the janizaries, after breaking the door down, and then a desperate fight followed on each story, the last defenders of the barracks being bayoneted on the roof, still fighting bravely. A battery which commanded the breach to a certain extent was stormed, the gunners standing by their pieces to the last. Part of the French storming column was now crushed by the fall of a tottering wall. At length the stormers reached a street, one of the largest in the town—nearly twelve feet wide, in fact. Here, however, they lost heavily under a fire from the walls and windows, and a large door barred their passage.

After an unsuccessful attempt to knock it down by main force, they sent for their powder carriers; but the Turks saved them further trouble by blowing it up themselves by accident. They had used this vaulted place for a powder store, and in the struggle a musket going off had set fire to some loose powder, and the whole exploded. Many of the stormers were killed or wounded by this explosion, and many were scorched all over, and their clothes completely burnt or blown off them.

The second party came up as the first received the full force of the explosion. The commander of the second column, Colonel Combe, carried his force forward through the destroyed door, and stormed a barricade beyond it. Here, mortally wounded, he handed over command of the stormers to the next senior officer, and slowly retired to where the Duc de Nemours and General Valée were standing. Here he politely expressed his happiness to have been able to strike a blow for King and country. The Duc, surprised at seeing him return alone from the scene of the fighting, asked him whether he was wounded. The old soldier proudly replied: ' No, sir; I am killed '; and true to his word, died.

A second barricade now barred the way of the French, and it was a difficult one to carry. It was formed of the French transport wagons abandoned in the retreat of the previous year. This barricade was also at length taken possession of by sapping through the neighbouring houses. By this time the besiegers had captured and opened the gate of El Djabia, and the third column now poured in. The chief men of the town then sent a letter offering to submit, and the fighting ceased. A large number of people are reported to have been driven in the struggle over a precipice 400 feet high into the ravines which border the town. This is explained by some to have been simply an attempted escape of the townspeople, who let themselves down by ropes over the wall, and that, startled by the sudden appearance of the French soldiers near at hand, some of the women imprudently jumped over the wall into the ravines below. Other authors mention this scene as a 'human avalanche' being hurled over the wall in the struggle. Probably the truth rests between the two extremes, and that, whilst some threw themselves over through fright, others were bayoneted and hurled over in the excitement of fighting. Large numbers of corpses were found here after the fighting. The Duc d'Orleans writes that 200 bodies were picked up at this fatal spot. He further accounts for the hard fighting at the storm by pointing out that the garrison largely outnumbered the *whole* of the French force, not to speak of the *storming* parties, and of course in street fighting in an Oriental town, such superiority in numbers was a great advantage.

The chief kaid or magistrate of the town had sworn not to be present at the capture of Constantine, and he kept his word by blowing his brains out before the surrender.

The desperate nature of the fighting may be judged by the number of killed and wounded amongst the French officers. The above-mentioned author gives the casualties in officers at this assault on the 13th of October as 23 killed and 57 wounded.

Order was re-established under the firm hand of General Valée, and three battalions only were allowed to garrison the town, whilst the remainder were withdrawn outside the city walls. A French officer was installed as governor of the place, and a prominent citizen was named chief magistrate of the native inhabitants. On the 17th of October a convoy arrived, escorted by three line battalions, bringing provisions. Unfortunately they also brought the cholera with them, and that at once broke out in the ranks of the army at Constantine, and thirty men died on the 18th of October alone. The chief of the Arabs living in a territory near Biskra came in on the 26th of October, and offered to catch the Bey of Constantine, whom he had long quarrelled with, and who was hiding in some mountains named Djebel Aurès, a district inhabited by Kabyles. The French gladly accepted his offer, and created him Aga of the Plains.

Leaving a garrison of some 2,500 men, cavalry and infantry, in the city, the remainder of the French force marched for Boné on the 29th of October, arriving there on the 3rd of November. There was no fighting on the homeward journey.

The losses of the French at the siege of Constantine are not fully reported; they must have been very heavy. In the assault alone 500 wounded were removed at its close to the hospitals.

General Valée was created a Marshal of France, and confirmed in his appointment as Governor-General of Algeria.

It is worthy of remark, as showing how much the French suffered from disease, that on the 20th of

November the sick at Boné numbered 1,300, despite the fact that 2,560 had just been sent away from the hospitals there to France. The reinforcements from France, however, had raised the strength of the French garrison in Algeria to just under 50,000 of all ranks.

CHAPTER XVI

No sooner had the French settled with the Bey of Constantine than they found new trouble brewing for them with Abd-el-Kader. This aspiring personage had decided to take full advantage of the Treaty of Tafna, and when any clause in this document appeared to be doubtful, he at once claimed the benefit of the doubt in most insolent language. A small colony of Coulouglis were peaceably settled at a place called Zeitoun, south-east of Algiers, and some sixty or seventy miles from it. These unfortunate people had accepted French control, and had received a kaid from the French—one of their own class, a Coulouglis. The Emir marched against them with 3,000 regular infantry, 400 regular cavalry, six guns, and some 11,000 Arabs. He easily destroyed this little colony fighting bravely to the end, and paraded the French-appointed kaid, sorely wounded and covered with blood, through his ranks, with every insult, and then killed him.

By a refinement of cruelty, Abd-el-Kader sent one of his regular battalions, composed largely of the Coulouglis of Tlemcen, first, to the attack on the Coulouglis of Zeitoun. He always bore a deadly hatred against these half-bred Turks of Tlemcen, on account of the gallant defence they had made against his forces, and it is to be feared that the 300

THE CONQUEST OF ALGERIA 141

Coulouglis in that regular battalion were not volunteers, but pressed men. It is some consolation to remember that though he could kill these unfortunate men, he could not break their spirit. Those who managed to escape from the massacre took refuge beside Algiers, and absolutely refused to join their co-religionists against the French; whilst the kaid, whom the Emir beheaded, bore himself proudly to the last, as if he were the victor and Abd-el-Kader the conquered enemy.

A strong French column moved out to the place, and the Emir withdrew. He still negotiated, but he was known to have said: 'Peace is made with the Christians only that true believers may prepare for further wars with them'; and every European saw that a war would be required to bring this arrogant man to reason.

Abd-el-Kader received some countenance from other European Powers at this time, and there is but little doubt that he was induced to use such haughty language to the French by the clever European adventurers who were in his camp. These men really made him believe that France would not be allowed to crush him, and that other European Powers, especially England and Russia, would intervene. On the 9th of February 1838, Lord Granville, English ambassador in Paris, presented a Note from his Foreign Office to the French Government, in which England strongly insisted that the sovereignty of the Algerian Territories really belonged to the Porte, and that France had not kept her word as to the promises she had made to the European Powers when the expedition sailed in 1830 against Algiers. He added that France could not be considered as exercising any other right than that of a military occupation of PART of the Regency of Algiers. This was bold language, but France well knew that it was not to be backed up by deeds, for at that time the English army and navy were few in numbers, and the people and government, labouring under the debt contracted in the Napoleonic wars, were not anxious to take any further steps beyond the use of threatening language. At the same time the French Government had their hands full, for a strong party in their own Parliament objected to the further extension of the conquest of Algeria, whilst Abd-el-Kader breathed war, and the French troops died in numbers from fever. More money and more troops had constantly to be poured into this sort of sieve with no apparent results.

In the province of Constantine everything went well for the French during 1838. Small expeditions went out, and in almost every case met with no opposition. The late Bey of Constantine, who was really a brave though cruel man, however, still led some marauders in the neighbouring mountains, and the French Aga of the Plains, the chief of the oasis of Biskra, instead of catching the Bey, as he had promised General Valée to do, was himself driven out of Biskra by him. General Valée would not allow any aid to be sent to his ally, so naturally the latter turned to Abd-el-Kader for assistance. A new road was opened from the sea to Constantine, viâ Stora (which place's name was changed to Philipville), El Arrouch, and Smendou, thus shortening the distance from the sea to Constantine by half; and

THE CONQUEST OF ALGERIA 143

other expeditions went as far as Mila, Setif, and Djémila. At the latter place some 600 French were besieged in December by many thousands of Kabyles during four days, but after a desperate resistance were relieved by the arrival of a French force, having lost fifty killed and wounded in the defence of the post.

In the Algiers province fortified camps were established by the governor at the foot of the hills thirty miles from the town, and Blida and Koléa were taken over by the French, and a garrison established beside them in fortified camps to watch them, as the inhabitants were anxious that no troops should be placed in these towns. During 1838 Abd-el-Kader was busy reducing a rival chief to reason. This man, also a marabout or saint, had refused to acknowledge the Emir as his chief, though quite willing to assist him against the French. The siege of his town lasted many months, and cost the Emir much loss of life and treasure. The name of the town was Ain Madhi, and it stood on the Sahara border of the province of Oran.

The Emir had thought that the mere sight of his arrival would have made his rival fly from his town of Ain Madhi. Here, however, he laboured under the same delusion as Marshal Clauzel at the first siege of Constantine. The enemy had absolutely no intention of flying. On the contrary, he thought himself much the stronger of the two, and when Abd-el-Kader arrived, escorted by some 400 of his regular horsemen and 1,800 regular infantry, and eighty artillerymen with two howitzers, he found that Mohammed-el-Tedjini, the saintly ruler of the desert town, was in no way dismayed at his arrival, but met his summons with the following proud reply, as quoted by M. Rousset :—

'Chief and Marabout,—I was a sultan when you were a baby. I do not understand what you wish here. I could quite understand if you asked for help to maintain or to undertake the Holy War, but on the contrary you have made a treaty with the infidels, and you now turn your arms against true Mahometans who have always agreed with you in all matters. You think we are feeble women; I will show you that we are lions, and all the blood which shall be shed in this encounter shall return upon *your* head.'

Abd-el-Kader was obliged for very shame's sake to undertake the siege of the place, but it was a particularly awkwardly situated town to capture. His supplies had to be brought to him from a long distance, or he had to raid the neighbouring tribes for food, which did not add to his popularity amongst them; whilst his enemy, securely sheltered behind his walls, lived in comparative peace and comfort despite all that Abd-el-Kader's artillerymen could do. The town was surrounded by palm-trees, and stood upon a small hill. It only consisted of a mosque, a citadel, and three hundred stone houses, but the walls of the town were twelve feet thick and twenty-seven feet high, and were flanked with towers, whilst both towers and walls were arranged to deliver a heavy musketry fire, being crenellated at the top. Inside, five wells supplied the necessary water for the garrison; and that garrison numbered some 900 fighting men, all well armed and fighting for their homes, and the place was stored with provisions. Outside the palm-

THE CONQUEST OF ALGERIA 145

trees and gardens, again, was a second wall, also flanked by towers. It was only fifteen feet high and not very thick, being pierced by loopholes for musketry fire.

The garrison soon justified the brave words of their chief. Abd-el-Kader arrived at Ain Madhi on the 18th of June 1838, and on the 1st of July, four small cannon that he had sent for when he perceived that he must besiege the place duly arrived. These opened a breach in the first walls by the 2nd of July, and the Emir at once sent his troops to storm the town.

The gardens and palm-trees were duly captured, with, however, a loss to the besiegers of 80 killed and 185 wounded. This was not very encouraging. Thirteen small cannon arrived, of which the two largest were 12-pounders, and it was only these two last that were the slightest use in battering down the wall. It shows the curious composition of the Emir's forces when it is noted that the officer commanding Abd-el-Kader's artillery was a Hungarian deserter from the Foreign Legion, whilst the Emir's private secretary, who did the engineering work of the attack, was a young Frenchman, named M. Leon Roches. After using up all his round shot, 800 in all, the wall still held firm, though sadly battered. Fortunately for the Emir, some mortars arrived from the Sultan of Morocco, and Marshal Valée, in the hopes of making a friend of Abd-el-Kader, supplied some bombs. Still the town held out, and, worse still, the neighbouring Arab tribe proceeded to pillage the convoy bringing food to the besiegers. This was, however, met by a counter raid which recovered the convoy and added to it all the herds of the wretched tribe. Then the besiegers tried mining the wall, but this was met by counter mines on the part of the besieged. Abd-el-Kader's prestige was on the wane. Many of the distant tribes refused to pay him tribute. He then had recourse to diplomacy. The agents of the Sultan of Morocco pointed out that both the leaders of besiegers and besieged were of the same faith, and should be directing their energies against the infidel, not against one another. Then ensued a strange arrangement. A truce was patched up for seven weeks, Mohammed-el-Tedjini and his men retired into the desert. Abd-el-Kader took the town, blew up some of its walls, and then retired. Honour was satisfied, still he had lost much time and men and money in the siege of this insignificant place.

He returned about the beginning of 1839 to Takdemt, which he now made his chief arsenal.

In May 1839 the French occupied Djidjeli with a Polish battalion of the Foreign Legion, and were immediately blockaded therein by the Kabyles, and the major of the battalion was killed. Abd-el-Kader in June traversed the whole of this country, no doubt stirring up ill feeling against the Christians.

Army reform now occupied Marshal Valée at Algiers, and it was under him that the natives were withdrawn by degrees from the Zouaves, and their places filled by Frenchmen, whilst the regiments of 'Turcos' or native riflemen were raised, beginning with a corps enrolled amongst the defenders of Constantine.

The Chasseurs d'Afrique, however, were somewhat

THE CONQUEST OF ALGERIA

differently arranged, as the corps was composed of Frenchmen, whilst one or two squadrons of natives were attached to the French squadrons as auxiliaries.

In July 1839 the Emperor of Morocco sent a robe of honour to Abd-el-Kader. It was presented to him in a solemn durbar, and then and there it was arranged that a Holy War against the infidels should be preached amongst the tribes, and that the Emir should give the signal when he considered the time favourable.

The favourable time came in this wise. The Duc d'Orleans came to Constantine, and Marshal Valée arranged that he should return by the direct road from Constantine to Algiers. This led through the mountains by a defile known as the 'Gates of Iron' ('Portes de Fer'). There were really two defiles, called the 'Great Gate' and the 'Little Gate,' both of which must be traversed. The force which was to be sent through was liable to be heavily attacked by the Kabyles. Therefore the report was spread that the troops were to be marched viâ Setif to Bougie. The Kabyles assembled on this route, and the French moved viâ Biban into the province of Algiers: 5,300 troops were assembled for this march, but only some 3,000 marched through the defile, the remainder returning to Constantine. The defile is described by one who made the march as following a watercourse between rock walls of 80 feet to 150 feet in height. He added that if a storm came on, the stream rose 20 feet to 25 feet in two hours. A storm did occur within half an hour of the last of the troops moving out of the defile, and if it had occurred whilst they were traversing it, all the men in the ravine would have been drowned. The gorge was some four miles long.

 The march through this pass was considered a great feat at the time by the French, and the following inscription was cut into one of the sides of the cliffs in the defile: 'Armée Française, 1839.' It certainly had a great effect upon the Kabyles, who, whilst the column remained for twenty-four hours at Setif, awaiting an improvement in the weather, sent in numerous chiefs to try and ascertain in what direction the marshal proposed to turn his steps. These chiefs were hospitably received and handsomely entertained, and a good glimpse of their treacherous character is afforded by the incident that one of these men, as he left the camp where he had been so well received, drew a pistol and shot, and killed, a corporal of the 2nd Light Infantry within one hundred yards of that camp.

 Such men could only be tamed by hard measures, as the French often found to their cost.

 It is said that the Romans, even when they owned Northern Africa, were very chary of using the Portes de Fer, as the hill tribes, even then, objected to any one passing through; and it will be remembered that the Bey of Constantine, when moving back from the siege of Algiers in 1830, with all the plunder he had taken from that province, was hunted through this pass by the Kabyles, who relieved him of most of his ill-gotten gains. The real importance of this pass, of course, arises from the fact that it is the shortest direct way from Algiers to Constantine, and that from Algiers it is only through it that access is obtained to the highlands of Mansoura towards Constantine,

THE CONQUEST OF ALGERIA 149

which stand some 1,100 feet above sea level. General Changarnier notes that three days before the French marched through, the water swirled along thirty feet deep in the road which the French Army used, as a result of the heavy rain. The marks were plainly visible on the walls of the defile, and, despite this abundance of water, much suffering was experienced by the troops, as all the streams are charged with magnesia, and the water is not, for that reason, suitable for drinking purposes.

The Arabs seized on this march as a reason for hostilities, and Abd-el-Kader fixed the 20th of November 1839 for the commencement. On the 10th of November, however, one of the tribes rose, and during the next ten days fire and sword swept all the French colonists from their homesteads, even within the circle of encampments before referred to. Many of the Arab tribes within this circle slipped out of it and joined their brethren in the fight. One detachment of French soldiers was annihilated, 108 men being killed.

Abd-el-Kader honourably warned Marshal Valée on the 18th of November that he must lead the tribes against the French.

From now on, constant fighting occurred. Blida had to be revictualled; 5,000 men were sent to cover the convoy. Even this large force was attacked, but the garrison of the fortified camp sallied out to assist, and the Arabs were driven off with a loss of ninety killed and wounded to the French.

On the 31st of December 1839 the governor-general, with 4,000 or 5,000 troops, marched towards Blida, which was still blockaded by the enemy. The

Arabs boldly advanced to meet him, bringing, besides many cavalry, three battalions of regular infantry and a gun.

This force was fiercely attacked by the French, glad to have this opportunity of closing with their wily enemy. The Arabs were driven away, their gun captured, and hundreds were killed, whilst the French lost 105 killed and wounded. The 2nd Light Infantry, as usual, led the charge, always first in attack and last in retreat.

Again, on the 29th of January, the 2nd Light Infantry went into action, and again broke up the enemy's regular battalions, losing themselves sixty-five men killed and wounded.

Whilst Abd-el-Kader was thus disturbing the province of Algiers, peace reigned in Oran, but during December 1839, various attempts at thefts and other outrages were made by the Arabs of that province. In February they attacked Misserghine, Arzeu, and Mazagran. All were beaten off. One example will show what these attacks consisted in. Mazagran was garrisoned by 123 men of the Regiment d'Afrique, which, it may be remembered, was composed of the various criminals of the army. Some 2,000 Arabs attacked them. After five days' fighting the enemy withdrew. The garrison lost nineteen men killed and wounded.

On the 12th of March yet another hard fight at Misserghine—some 800 French in all against thousands of Arabs. The French loss was over 100; the Arabs, as usual, were defeated.

In the province of Constantine Abd-el-Kader was not paramount. His lieutenant was attacked by a

THE CONQUEST OF ALGERIA

local tribe and 500 of his men were killed. The French conferred the Legion of Honour on the chief of this tribe as well as £1,700. A well-conducted raid against another hostile tribe supplied some 80,000 head of camels, cattle, and sheep, and brought that tribe to a more humble temper, whilst an attack made by the Arabs on the 62nd Regiment near Setif was handsomely beaten off after five days' skirmishing.

The French Army in Algeria was now raised to 60,000 men by fresh regiments from France and by drafts sent to the other regiments in the country. Some cases of piracy having occurred at Cherchel, about 5,000 or 6,000 troops were sent there between the 12th and the 21st of March. The town was found to be deserted, but was seized and garrisoned by the French, and then the columns were sent home, having lost some sixty-two killed and wounded in various skirmishes on the way. The Duc d'Orleans arrived from France on the 13th of April 1840 to join the army for the attack on Abd-el-Kader, and was accompanied by the Duc d'Aumale, his brother.

The forces that Abd-el-Kader could bring against the French as made up by the French Staff were, some 5,000 Infantry, 1,000 Cavalry, and 150 gunners. Besides these regular troops he had some 50,000 irregular horsemen, and of course many irregular foot soldiers of sorts. He was supposed to have £60,000 of ready money in his treasury, and was known to have five small arsenals, viz. Takdemt, Boghar, Taza, Saida, and Tafraona, all situated on the northern edge of the Sahara, well out of the reach of the French at present.

Forming a corps of some 10,000 men, Marshal Valée crossed the Chiffa on the 27th of April 1840. Undismayed by the large French force, the Arabs promptly attacked that afternoon, and were charged four times by all the cavalry and were attacked fiercely by the Zouaves and 2nd Light Infantry before they were beaten back. On the 29th Abd-el-Kader appeared, escorted by 10,000 cavalry, and leisurely rode round the French Army. Particularly notable was his bodyguard, all dressed in red. The French Army wandered rather aimlessly about until the 12th of May, when it moved up and attacked the pass of Mouzaia, on the way to Medea. Three columns attacked this pass, which Abd-el-Kader defended in person with all his troops, which had been well entrenched by European deserters. After a stiff struggle the defile was carried with a loss to the French of 300 killed and wounded, of whom 200 belonged to the 2nd Light Infantry. During the engagement the convoy had been halted at the bottom of the pass. On the 17th of May the town of Medea was occupied. It was found to be deserted, and a garrison of some 2,400 men were at once installed, the garrison provisioned and the place made defensible, and on the 20th of May the army moved back over the pass, which had been guarded in the interval by two infantry battalions.

The Emir attacked the French rearguard in an olive wood before arriving at the pass. A very hard struggle ensued, as the rearguard only numbered three battalions, and the Arabs, besides 50,000 horsemen, had three battalions of regular infantry in the field. The Arab horsemen dismounted and fought on foot

THE CONQUEST OF ALGERIA 153

with their long flintlocks. The rearguard being reinforced by a Zouave battalion attacked in turn and drove off the Arabs, and the army crossed the pass in peace. The French loss on this day was 350 killed and wounded. The Duc d'Orleans returned to France after this expedition.

On the 4th of June the Marshal again moved out with his column and marched to Miliana. On the 8th of June, after a show of defence, the French Army marched into Miliana, which was deserted and in flames. On the 12th of June the army moved out again, leaving a garrison of 1,200 men in the town. The French marched towards Medea, being attacked on the way by the Emir, who was severely punished, especially by the French cavalry. The losses on the side of the Europeans were 124 men killed and wounded on this day. The pass of Mouzaia was seized during the night of 14th–15th of May by a party of infantry without fighting, but next day, the 15th of May, whilst the convoy and rearguard moved towards the pass, it was again attacked in the olive wood by the Emir. This time they were most boldly charged by the French, and driven from the field with heavy loss. The French lost that day in wounded alone, not counting killed, 380 men. The wounded were transported on the 16th to Blida by the cavalry, which then brought back a fresh convoy for Medea. The infantry in the meantime camped near the pass and rested. On the 21st of June Medea was revictualled, and on the 22nd a convoy was sent on to Miliana under command of Colonel Changarnier, the commanding officer of the 2nd Light Infantry, who was supplied with 4,000 men.

The senior officers were exceedingly jealous of his being chosen to command, but it must be acknowledged that he thoroughly deserved his position. By feigning to march towards the pass of Mouzaia, Colonel Changarnier induced the Emir to place his troops in this place, and by the evening of the 24th of June his convoy of 60,000 rations was delivered in Miliana, and he was ready to return just as Abd-el-Kader's foot-soldiers came up by forced marches to attack him. On closer inspection, however, the Arabs decided to leave him alone, and only observed him from afar on his march back to Medea. Colonel Changarnier was duly promoted after his return from this expedition. The troops then marched back to their camps near Algiers. An unhealthy summer followed and decimated the French Army, which numbered some 72,000 men.

How deadly the climate was, is best shown by remarking that 5,000 were in hospital on the 1st of November 1840, that 4,200 men had died since the 1st of June, whilst 2,700 had been returned as invalids since the same date to France.

A convoy was sent from Blida to Medea at the end of August under General Changarnier. It found everything in capital order, and that one attack only had been made by the enemy on the 3rd of July, which had been repulsed, though with a loss to the garrison of 145 killed and wounded. This convoy on its return ambuscaded some of Abd-el-Kader's regulars who pursued the rearguard with more valour than discretion, and over a hundred dead bodies were left on the ground as the result of one bayonet charge by the French. On the 19th of September once again

THE CONQUEST OF ALGERIA 155

General Changarnier moved out to relieve fifty men in a fort at Kara Moustafa besieged by the Arabs. Taking 1,800 men, with three days' provisions, he surprised the enemy's outposts, rushed their infantry camp before dawn, and boldly attacked their cavalry, some 1,300 strong with three squadron of Chasseurs d'Afrique, only supporting them with infantry. The Arabs lost 130 killed and 17 prisoners, whilst the French lost only 20 men killed and wounded.

At the end of September Miliana ran short of provisions and was reprovisioned by a convoy taken there by General Changarnier, who left 1,200 fresh men as a garrison, and brought back the old garrison greatly broken down by their summer in the blockaded town. The French loss in this affair was some 300 killed and wounded. The old garrison was so debilitated by their experiences that by the end of the year out of 1,236 who had formed the garrison of Miliana only 70 survived. Marshal Valée was now recalled to France, and General Bugeaud was made governor-general in his place.

Little of importance had taken place in the provinces of Constantine and Oran. In the first the French had held their own. In the latter they had towards the close of the year instituted a series of raids, which had resulted in great captures of live stock and women from the hostile tribes. The friendly natives plucked up heart, and the French soldiers began to despise their enemies now that they had found their weak point out.

CHAPTER XVII

GENERAL BUGEAUD was determined to reduce Algeria to submission, and the Government ably seconded his measures by raising his army from 61,000 men to 78,000 men. He determined to bring the enemy to terms by attacking him with 'flying' columns. Instead of sending great columns to escort convoys to places like Miliana or Medea, he decided that these places only existed for the purpose of forming depôts at which the fighting forces could fill up with stores, so that the act of supplying these places with provisions, which before had been the great event of the war, so soon as possible should go on as a sort of secondary matter; and though the convoys had to pass frequently to and fro, they would be guarded in ordinary course by some troops detailed for the purpose, whilst the beating up of the Arab quarters beyond Medea and Miliana should keep them so busy that they would not have much spare time to assemble for the purpose of cutting up the convoys. Harassed as usual by want of transport, the general ordered that the cavalry should march with the columns dismounted, leading their horses, each of which carried a bag of grain across the saddle. Needless to say, a great outcry was made, but it was a sensible order.

First, in April 1841 two trips with a convoy were

THE CONQUEST OF ALGERIA 157

made to Medea. The loss of the French in the first was 231 killed and wounded. The second convoy was not interfered with by the enemy. In the beginning of May, whilst taking supplies to Miliana, the French were met by Abd-el-Kader with 20,000 men. On the 3rd of May only a slight skirmish occurred, in which the enemy lost about 100 killed. On the 4th of May a great cavalry combat was fought, chiefly with regulars, &c., led by Abd-el-Kader, who were only driven from the field by the utmost exertions of the French cavalry, whilst immediately afterwards many thousands of mounted Arabs, divided into two bodies, appeared. One drawn from the eastern tribes was commanded by an Arab called Barkani, whilst the western tribes had as commander Ben Arach. These irregulars were easily driven back. Small skirmishes in May nearer Algiers had cost the French some 40 men killed.

Then, leaving General Baraguey d'Hilliers in charge of a column 7,000 strong in the province of Algiers, with orders to destroy Boghar and Taza, General Bugeaud went himself to Mostaganem to meet Lamoricière, who had also a strong column waiting to proceed with the general to destroy Takdemt. A few light cannon were taken—three 12-pounders. The French had learnt wisdom from their failure at Constantine.

As the way was unknown, a captain named Martimprey had been directed to make as accurate a map as possible of the country from reports of natives. His map was found to be most correct, and he led the way with a flag, and was promptly nick-named 'The Polar Star' by the sharp little

French infantrymen. Leaving Mostaganem on the 18th of May, Takdemt was reached on the 25th, after a peaceable journey. The place was burning, and Abd-el-Kader was sitting with an army on the hills watching. The French blew up the fort and moved to Mascara, skirmishing the whole way with the Arabs. Mascara was also deserted, but not destroyed. Leaving a garrison there, the French returned by another route to Mostaganem. This route, from Mascara to Mostaganem, leads across the mountains, and this column lost 60 men in the ravines from Kabyle skirmishers.

By the 3rd of June the French were back at Mostaganem, and by the 10th of June had brought an enormous convoy to Mascara, whilst the garrison of that place had sallied out and had reaped the enemy's crops and brought them in. In the province of Algiers these two places, Boghar and Taza, were both destroyed by General Baraguey d'Hilliers, so Abd-el-Kader's arsenals were now reduced to Saida and Tafraona, also known as Sebdou. In July the French lost 120 killed and wounded in an engagement near Mascara, but beat off the Arabs under Abd-el-Kader. In September, again, the governor-general was near Mascara fighting Abd-el-Kader, who had produced some 9,000 men. On the 8th of October heavy fighting took place between some 1,800 French cavalry and the Emir's horsemen. The French cavalry had to be supported in haste by the Zouaves, or they would have been cut up. The French moved about the country south of Mascara, destroying the crops and the huts of the hostile tribes; then, marching south some ninety miles, they destroyed Saida, another arsenal of the Emir's, leaving him only one in working order. South of Saida the French found some pastoral tribes hostile to Abd-el-Kader. They offered to lead them to the place where the inhabitants of the town of Saida were in hiding, but on the arrival of the troops they were found to have fled. A fight, however, took place with the Emir's bodyguard, which was handsomely beaten and their standards carried away. This expedition lasted altogether fifty-three days.

All through the autumn of 1841 the raiding and fighting went on. Led by Arab deserters, the French found their enemy's supplies in 'silos,' or holes in the ground already described, and the dates and grain were steadily transferred to Mascara to increase the supplies of that depôt. A radius of seventy miles round Mascara was kept clear of the enemy by constant night marches, which at first resulted in great seizures of cattle, sheep, and donkeys. The good effects of this activity were soon apparent. The tribes between Mascara and Mostaganem came in, and convoys were now able to pass freely to Mascara with but small escorts. In February 1842, Tafraona, the last of the Emir's arsenals, was destroyed. It lay near the Morocco frontier; and after viewing its destruction from afar, Abd-el-Kader went over into Morocco for safety.

Tlemcen was also occupied during the same month, and agriculture commenced to flourish round the various posts held by the French. Still the raids went on, the French power always growing. Thus in February some sixty villages of tents or huts were swept up in one day, counting some 6,000 people, with all their cattle. The tribes steadily came in to the French, and Abd-el-Kader was reduced to raiding over the Morocco border. At the end of April he was caught up by a force from Tlemcen and escaped, leaving 200 killed and 70 prisoners. As in Oran, so in the province of Algiers. The columns moved ever farther away from the towns, destroying crops, &c., and bringing the waverers to the French side. It was not done without loss, but the French troops had recognised that they were the conquering race. For instance, a small party of twenty-one French were called upon to surrender by some hundreds of Arabs. They were not entrenched, but were marching in the open. As they refused to yield, they were vigorously attacked, but held out as vigorously under a sergeant named Blandan. He was soon mortally wounded, and sixteen others were killed or wounded; but the remainder fought on manfully, and were relieved at the last gasp by some French cavalry attracted by the sound of firing. The raids increased their length so much that at last, on the 30th of May 1842, the column from Oran met the column from Algiers near the banks of the Chélif river. One tribe who refused to surrender retired into extensive caves in some mountains, and time was lacking to starve them out.

On the 5th of June 1842, after a skirmish, the name of Adjutant Major d'Aurelle de Paladines was specially mentioned in orders for good work accomplished. It is interesting to recall that the only Frenchman who won a battle against the Germans in the war of 1870-71 bore this name.

Whilst these operations were going on in Algeria

it is instructive to find that some members of the French Parliament suggested that the plain south of Algiers should be surrounded by a ditch guarded by blockhouses, and that the French should only occupy this amount of land. General Bugeaud's sensible remark on the subject was that such a ditch would be useful to drain the marshy ground, but was liable to give fever to at least 1,000 soldiers a month. In June, near Miliana, the French lost forty-three men killed in a skirmish. On the 1st of July 1842, General Changarnier crossed the last of the Atlas Mountains towards the south, and saw at his feet, looking south, the plateau of Sersou, with the Nahr Ouassel river running at his feet. No French column had gone as far south as this, so far, but he noticed more particularly great clouds of dust on the plain. He realised it must be some of the irreconcilable tribes flying before him, and, pushing on some ten miles with his cavalry, picked up 3,000 prisoners and 15,000 head of cattle. Again, later on, further west, the French drove some tribes down south upon the salt lakes called Chott-el-Chergui. Here large numbers surrendered, whilst others crossed the shallow lake, many being swallowed up in its treacherous waters and muddy bottom. These flying tribes gathered together to the number of 30,000, and moved south across the plateau of Sersou, pursued by the French. Many tribes of the south rallied to the French. On one occasion it is noted that from one hostile tribe's silos alone 8,000 camel-loads of grain were taken. During the year 1842 the divisions of Mascara passed some 300 days actually in the field in pursuit of the enemy. Abd-el-Kader retaliated by destroying El Bordj and Frenda, small towns east of Mascara, but his visits to this part of the world were brief and troubled.

These small expeditions continued, always with much loss to the enemy—generally with small loss to the French. What the losses to the enemy were is best shown by an example. A chief of a hostile tribe, coming in to make terms, said quite naturally, ' I had eight sons: six are dead, fighting against you.'

These tribes, of course, were largely sustained by their religion, which made the war a holy one, and also by the fact that if the said six sons had not been killed fighting the French, they would probably have been killed in local squabbles against their neighbours, as the whole country was always a seething mass of broils and local or tribal feuds. The French, as said above, had their losses also. On the 19th and 20th of September, for instance, a column under Colonel Cavaignac lost 144 men killed and wounded, out of some 2,000 men, under an attack from the Kabyles in some mountains far south of Medea.

That these people were well armed was also a fact, as the French proved early when disarming the tribes. For instance, a tribe named the Ouled Aziz, being granted a protection, was ordered to deliver up 600 muskets, and did so without any trouble. Probably it could not have turned out 2,000 warriors, or anything like that number; and no doubt many muskets were retained. The powder was obtained from Morocco and from Abd-el-Kader, from Tunis and from the sea-coast, where small sailing boats used to bring it from Tangier, Gibraltar, &c.

On the 19th of November 1842 the Duc d'Aumale

THE CONQUEST OF ALGERIA 163

returned to Africa. He became Governor of Medea, and took the field in charge of a column of 3,000 men. Two other columns worked with him. The Duc's formed the right, the centre column was 2,000 strong, and the left one numbered 2,700 men. These three columns worked through a range of mountains south and a little west of Miliana, which range was much sought after by Abd-el-Kader and his friends. To support these columns yet a fourth one was formed, which moved out from Miliana and established a depôt of provisions near the range so that the columns could replenish their stores without long marches to the towns. These little depôts were christened by the wags of the French Army 'Biscuitville,' and of course were most useful. The enemy, nothing loath for a fight, concentrated on the left column, and for four days, from the 8th to the 12th of December, fought desperately with it, cutting off part of a mountain battery. The three columns rejoined, and on the 18th of December returned to the country where the fighting had taken place, and by dint of destroying everything, and capturing flocks and women and children, brought the tribesmen to submission. No sooner had the troops retired, about the end of December 1842, than Abd-el-Kader reappeared, fell upon the submitted tribesmen, beheaded some of the chiefs and sent others in chains to his encampment, away in the south-west. The whole of the tribes thus harried rose in revolt against the French. Columns had to move everywhere from the 20th of January 1843 to the end of March, by which time most of the tribes had been again compelled to submit, and Abd-el-Kader had again disappeared.

On the 11th of May 1843 a hostile tribe emigrating to join Abd-el-Kader ran into the column of Colonel Pelissier. Nothing daunted, the Arabs pointed out that they had already submitted to some other column, and were permitted to pass. Finding, however, that their statement was incorrect, they were pursued and brought back as prisoners with all their flocks, some 2,000 prisoners alone being taken, whilst the neighbouring tribes came in in large numbers next day. Some other tribes retired to the top of a plateau surrounded by cliffs and prepared to defend themselves, more troops arrived and they were blockaded, and running short of water had to surrender. Again 2,000 prisoners and many herds, &c., were taken.

On the 16th of May 1843 the Chasseurs d'Afrique, to the number of 110, chasing a flying column, ran into 1,500 mounted Arabs. They were relieved by some infantry some hours later, after losing in the fighting fifty-two killed and wounded.

On the same day the Duc d'Aumale, who had been pursuing Abd-el-Kader's camp with a column of 2,000 men, came upon them with his cavalry, some 500 strong, at a place called Taguine. He very bravely at once galloped down on the camp, and, despite the fact that there were 5,000 fighting men against him, captured 3,000 out of 10,000 people present, recovered the prisoners carried off by Abd-el-Kader as hostages from the tribes friendly to France, took all the flocks, and killed 300 of the enemy, losing 21 men himself. Abd-el-Kader's harem managed to escape, but the blow to his prestige was immense.

This very gallant attack, though apparently foolhardy, was a necessity. If the French had attempted to retreat they would have been fallen upon by the enemy and probably annihilated. Their only chance was to impress the enemy with the belief that all their infantry was within call, and they were successful in making him believe this. Some 1,500 infantry, of course, were hastening up to support the cavalry, but they were miles away across the sandy plain, and would have required much time to have got up to the scene of the fight.

The flying mob ran into another French column from Miliana, and many were taken prisoners. The friendly Arabs of the Douair and Sméla tribes carried off so much plunder from this raid that on their way home they were attacked by some of the recently submitted tribes, and their chief was killed. He was a most gallant man, was named Moustafa, and had been created a general by the French; and well deserved the rank. Foremost in every fight, he was killed in this one, leading a gallant charge with few men against overwhelming numbers. He was given a military funeral according to his army rank by the French, and his nephew was created chief of the tribe in his place. Abd-el-Kader, ever active and energetic, within a month had tried to recoup his losses by plundering a tribe friendly to the French. His captures from them were immense, and he withdrew, leaving several tribes with the booty guarded by some of his bodyguard and a battalion of regulars, all slowly withdrawing towards the south-west. General Lamoricière fell upon this party of emigrants at a place some hundred miles nearly due east from Mostaganem, and after hard fighting drove them in great confusion into the arms of General Bugeaud.

Again many hostile Arab tribes surrendered and received protection from the French.

On the 22nd of June 1843 Colonel Gery surprised the Emir's camp. His men had made a trying march the day before of some thirty miles, but moving off again at one in the morning, they covered eighteen miles by six o'clock. The cavalry charged the camp half an hour before, and a stubborn fight ensued, which was ended by the arrival of the infantry, who promptly attacked and destroyed the enemy's line. The Arabs lost very heavily: 250 dead bodies were left on the field, and, according to Arab custom, many more were carried away by their fellow-countrymen. Great numbers of arms, camels, &c., were also taken. Yet on the 30th the Emir was again in the field, this time trying to carry Mascara by a sudden and unexpected attack. Fortunately the French garrison, some 300 strong, received him bravely, and the attack failed. General Bugeaud came up with a column, followed the Emir, and tried to surprise him on the night of the 3rd and 4th of July, but failed, and Abd-el-Kader after a hard fight was able to make his retreat. He promptly replied by attacking a French working party between Mascara and Oran, but these men, some 250 strong, hastily built some stone sangars and beat him off. These repeated attacks of Abd-el-Kader had to be met somehow. General Bugeaud decided to meet them with mounted infantry. His first attempt at this new force was to mount 700 men of the 33rd Regiment on mules. The French infantry were quite pleased at this novelty, and it was a great success. The equipment was primitive: owing to a scarcity of bridles, the

THE CONQUEST OF ALGERIA 167

halters of the mules were made to do duty, and WOODEN bits were made for them; the pack saddle was used to ride upon, with small boards tied up with cords as stirrups. Besides the soldier the mules also carried twelve days' rations for their rider, four days' rations of corn for themselves, enough firewood to last two days, and a gallon of water. The mules must have been very heavily weighted, but we do not hear of any complaints on that score. In case of attack the men worked in threes: No. 2 held the mules whilst Nos. 1 and 3 fought. The first raid made by the mounted infantry was a great success. The mounted infantry, strengthened by the addition of some Zouaves, was over 1,000 strong, and was supported by 500 cavalry, whilst 800 camels followed as a convoy. The first march was some fifty-four miles without a long halt. Some tribes having refused to give hostages for their good behaviour were surprised on the morning of the 4th of August 1843 after a thirty-six mile night march, and as a result of a close pursuit and capture of all their herds these tribes promptly came to terms. General Bugeaud was created a marshal in July 1843.

During August and September several attempts were made by night marches to surprise the Emir's camp. Twice it was rushed at dawn, but each time the outposts gave warning, and the Emir with most of his forces slipped away. Upon one occasion, however, he returned the compliment by decoying the Chasseurs d'Afrique to attack a small column of regular infantry, whilst he charged them unobserved with 400 cavalry from a flank. Very heavy fighting ensued, but the Arabs were finally driven off. A French trumpeter, having given up his horse to his captain in this fight, was taken prisoner by the enemy; but the Emir, respecting his bravery, treated him well, and the French Legion of Honour having been sent to the trumpeter whilst still a prisoner, he paraded his regulars to witness the presentation and afterwards exchanged him.

On the 6th of November 1843, Abd-el-Kader's regular infantry succumbed after a splendid fight. Attacked by some 1,300 French, these brave men formed a square, and, though greatly outnumbered, marched with flags flying and drums beating towards a small rocky hill, where they hoped to secure a good position and so to hold off the enemy until nightfall should give them some chance of escape. The square was finally broken, and after losing their two majors commanding the battalions, 18 captains, and 380 men killed, the remainder surrendered, consisting of some 13 officers and 270 men. No doubt some few managed to escape, but practically the whole were killed or taken. The officer commanding the whole force was killed in the following manner. When his column was broken up he fled, but, being attacked, killed a corporal who pursued him, then the horse of his next pursuer, and wounded the next man who attacked him, and was promptly shot by a fourth. The French gave Ben Allai—for such was the gallant man's name—a general's military funeral, burying him in his family ground at Kolea. Abd-el-Kader was absent at the time with some 200 of his mounted body-guard. He appeared on the field of battle so soon as the French quitted it, buried his men's bodies, and then retired again with his remaining fighting forces and the non-combatants into Morocco.

THE CONQUEST OF ALGERIA 169

At the end of 1843 the Emir again appeared with 500 men, and raided as far as Tlemcen, but was attacked by the Arab tribes, and hastily retired over the border into Morocco.

In the province of Constantine during 1842 and 1843 many small expeditions had been undertaken with the usual results, viz. that many tribes surrendered, others migrated, many natives were killed and some French soldiers. In May and June 1842, two small columns lost 65 and 70 killed and wounded respectively. The latter loss was out of a force only 200 strong. These expeditions were carried on round Constantine itself. The great mass of mountains south of Dellys to Djedjilli, known as Grande Kabylie, was barely touched; and, in fact, was not conquered until 1857.

The Duc d'Aumale became governor of the province of Constantine in December 1843, and in March took an expedition to the south to establish a garrison at Batna, and to clear out many hostile tribes who interfered with caravans coming up from the south to trade with the French. L'Aures, a mountainous district in that part of the world, was also visited, and after a slight repulse, the Kabyles of this district were trained into a more peaceable frame of mind. A few days previously a small fortified village had been carried by storm by the French. It was some twenty-five miles from Biskra, and besides its own garrison was helped by some Kabyles, who lined the mountain crests and assisted in the defence by rolling large rocks down on the French as they moved forward to assault the village. After a day's heavy fighting this village was carried.

On the 8th of April 1844 Ahmed Bey, the

late Bey of Constantine, was unfortunate enough to have his camp rushed by the French, who chased him manfully until the 13th of April. The Arabs whom he was with surrendered on that day, whilst the Bey retired farther south and escaped.

In May 1844 a French column moved to Ain Madhi, which will be remembered as the town which gave Abd-el-Kader such a hard fight before he was able to enter it some years earlier. The column marched from Medea via Taguine, and was noticeable as having consisted of mounted infantry on camels. Two men were told off to each camel, but one walked whilst the other rode, alternately. The column calculated on marching forty miles a day, and carried thirty days' provisions on the mounted infantry camel, so was very self-contained. At Ain Madhi there was some trouble about the entry of the column, as the chief of the town said that he would lose his holy character with his own people if any infidels were permitted to enter. However, instead of the whole column some eleven officers were admitted, and when the taxes were paid they were returned to the chief, so the French and he parted great friends.

It is worthy of notice that the French complain that their great difficulty in dealing with the submitted tribes was to find a suitable man to establish as chief over them, for Abd-el-Kader had always a rival chief appointed, and the French, much against their will, had to agree that he had appointed the most suitable man, and that they were obliged to chose only the second best.

An expedition was also made by Marshal Bugeaud in May 1844. He took three columns with him from

THE CONQUEST OF ALGERIA

Algiers and pushed into the hills south of Dellys, which seaport he used as a base to supply his troops from. The Kabyles fought well, and on one occasion caused him a loss of 137 killed and wounded. Finally, however, the main tribes, especially the 'Flitta,' surrendered. It was on this expedition that an interesting diary was written by an officer in the Zouaves. He describes the rocky nature of the country, the outraging of a young Kabyle girl by two of the African Light Infantry, and finally mentions how the Kabyles took some of the friendly natives prisoners, and how the whole of the camp was horrified at night by these wretched creatures being roasted to death by their cruel enemies, so close to the camp that their shrieks could be heard, but on the verge of such an impassable precipice that it was impossible to intervene and save them.

Marshal Bugeaud, however, had not time to carry this expedition to a satisfactory conclusion, for on the 20th of May he had received dispatches which brought him news that matters were threatening in the Province of Oran. How serious he thought the news to be may be gathered from his despatch to Marshal Soult, Minister of War at Paris, as quoted by M. Rousset.

He wrote, as he was embarking hastily at Dellys to go to Oran, as follows:—

'What I desire from the Almighty before everything, is that our enemies may temporise long enough to give me time to join General Lamoricière' (in the Province of Oran).

Things must have been very black indeed before this hardy old warrior, called 'Father' Bugeaud by his troops, could write in such a strain.

CHAPTER XVIII

WHEN Abd-el-Kader retired into Morocco after his unsuccessful raid of the 23rd of December 1843, he proceeded to recruit his forces. The border tribes were nothing loath to joining him, but owing to fear of the French, the Sultan of Morocco did his best to prevent them doing so. However, more and more of these wild cavaliers joined the Emir, and, finally, even the tribes who officially guarded the border threw in their lot with him. Marshal Bugeaud then sent a column forward from Mascara, with orders to establish a post on the upper branches of the Tafna, a river which runs into the Isser, or Issus, mentioned by Fénelon in 'Telemachus' as flowing over 'golden' sands. This post was named Lalla Maghnia. The reason for this movement was an attack on a French party in which two men were killed, and amongst the assailants was recognised the uniform, such as it was, of the before-mentioned guardians of the border.

In March 1844, Abd-el-Kader raided some Arab tribes between Mascara and Sidi Bel Abbes. The French general, Lamoricière, at once moved down to the Tafna, and having warned the nearest Moorish governor of his intentions, proceeded to erect the fort of Lalla Maghnia on French or Algerian ground. The Moorish governor, or Lord of the Marches, objected, saying he had no orders on the subject, but a

THE CONQUEST OF ALGERIA 173

passable fort was made by the French, and the column, some 4,500 strong, encamped beside it. On the 28th of May 1844 the column, leaving a garrison in the fort, moved up to within some six miles of the frontier. On the 30th of May, without further parley, the enemy advanced in good order to the attack. The French had just time to strike their camp and move out to receive him. The fight was short, and ended in the complete defeat of the Moors. The French settled down under Lalla Maghnia, and awaited the arrival of Marshal Bugeaud, who came on the 12th of June with some 2,500 additional troops. On the 15th the Moorish governor came to an interview with a French general, sent as a sort of envoy. The interview was broken up in the middle for three-quarters of an hour, by the Moorish soldiers pressing upon the French officers, and shouting threats and insults at them, but, being resumed, was finally broken off by the Moor demanding that the French should consent to their boundary being now marked by the Tafna. As they declined to move it back from the old Turkish frontier, he quietly intimated that they would fight for it.

As the envoys returned, the Moorish soldiery opened fire upon them, and then fought with the rearguard of the small escort protecting the French ambassadors. Fortunately retribution overtook these ruffians at once: for the hunted flag of truce fell back on a stronger body of French, and Marshal Bugeaud moved up with four battalions to their support. The cavalry charged, and the Moors broke and fled. The French Native Cavalry raised a pyramid of 150 heads cut from the fallen. The Marshal next day marched over the frontier into Morocco and took a small

Moorish town called Oudjda. It had a population of some 5,000 people, most of whom, however, fled on the approach of the French.

Abd-el-Kader improved the occasion by slipping round the French left into the province of Oran, but, finding a column watching for him at Saida, decided to move back again. He had already recruited some 2,000 mounted men, many of them being regular troops from Morocco.

The French now opened another harbour on the coast, called by them Nemours, though known to the Moors by the Arabic equivalent of 'The Mosque of the Pirates.' This reduced their line of communication to some thirty miles only, which, of course, made a great difference to the transport of provisions, &c.

The French Marshal offered to march on Fez, the capital of Morocco, if he were permitted to take 20,000 infantry and 2,000 cavalry. Fez is stated by Colonel Scott to have then contained 300,000 inhabitants, of whom 20,000 were Jews. Fortunately wiser counsels prevailed. The French equipped a fleet under the command of the Prince de Joinville, and sent it to Tangier to demand an apology for the repeated attacks on their army, and further demanded that Abd-el-Kader should no longer be given a refuge in Moorish territory. The Moors only replied that they wished Lalla Maghnia to be destroyed and Marshal Bugeaud punished. On the 6th of August 1844 the Prince de Joinville opened fire on the fortifications of Tangier, and in three hours destroyed them. The Moors lost 550 killed and wounded, the fleet only 19.

THE CONQUEST OF ALGERIA 175

The French fleet then sailed for Mogador on the west of Morocco. Here the fleet bombarded the forts on the 15th of August, and landed some 500 men, who destroyed the forts and established this party as a garrison on a small island in the port. The Kabyles or Berbers came down from the mountains and assisted the French, no doubt unwittingly, by looting the houses of Mogador. This place was particularly chosen for attack as the emperor was the actual owner and landlord of the place, receiving even the rents of any houses which might be let. Thus he was very heavily hit in his pocket, but whilst this was going on, the Moorish Army was receiving one of its many beatings from a European foe. Some two miles west of Oudjda runs the river of Isly. Here the Moors assembled a large army, a fair proportion of whom were regulars, amongst them the black mounted bodyguard of the Emperor of Morocco.

Colonel Scott, with reference to this bodyguard of the emperor, gives the following details. Europeans, who managed to escape from the Spanish settlements of Ceuta and Mililah, and who were lucky enough to get as far south as Fez, were made to enter the bodyguard. The colonel was informed whilst in Morocco that there were 6,000 soldiers in this bodyguard who claimed to be Europeans, being either French or Spanish deserters. In many cases, however, they were sent to a town south of Fez, and forty-eight miles distant from it, named Ligouri. Here they were formed into regiments, and officers were selected from themselves. They were given wives and lands, and were paid twelve shillings a month, and became military settlers, somewhat after the manner of the Russian military villages. He further adds that those men who managed to reach Fez were esteemed as fortunate, for the Moorish chiefs *en route* made a practice of arresting these unfortunates, and of selling them as slaves to whoever would buy them at the rate of twelve or sixteen shillings each. Of course, it must be remembered that Ceuta was a penal settlement, and therefore the men escaping from it were probably thorough scamps, and were not considered as desirable neighbours even by a Moorish chief. Whether it was true that there were anything like 6,000 Europeans in the bodyguard is open to question. One thing, however, is certain, and that is that they did not come down to fight the French on this occasion, as the only mention made anywhere is of the negroes and other natives in the guard. Probably it was considered that if the Europeans had been sent, they might have treacherously turned on the Moorish Army and have helped the French to give it a thorough beating.

The French received a reinforcement of four squadrons from France on the 12th of August, and the army now consisted of 8,500 infantry, 1,400 cavalry, and 16 guns, with some 400 native irregulars. On the 13th of August the force moved out at three o'clock in the afternoon, bivouacked for the night without fires, moved again at two a.m., forded the river Isly, and moved quietly up the left bank, thus interposing between the enemy's camp on the right bank and his line of retreat. As the sun rose the Moorish camp came into view, with the soldiers hastily arming.

They were not taken by surprise, as the French had been bickering with some mounted scouts all the night on the left bank. The French formed for battle in three brigades in a somewhat curious formation, described as a 'lozenge,' and then, with bands playing, marched on the enemy, fording the Isly again on the way.

It may be remarked that the 'lozenge' was really a series of echelons flanking one another. A great cloud of dust arose as the forces met, and the Moors very bravely tried to break each separate battalion. They lost enormously from the French fire, and then the cavalry were let loose on them. In a short time the camp was in the hands of the French, with all the Moorish guns, to the number of eleven. Some of the French cavalry were surrounded by enormous numbers of the enemy, and would have been roughly handled, but three infantry battalions drove off the enemy. This was really the only phase of the battle which caused the French Marshal any anxiety. This French cavalry managed to become separated from the rest of the army, and seeing the danger they were in, as the enemy had recognised their isolated position, the infantry was rushed to their assistance as fast as the men could run.

By noon the fighting ceased; 120 men were killed and wounded on the French side, whilst the Moors left 800 dead on the field. Their numbers were uncertain, but they were understood to have had 30,000 mounted men and 10,000 infantry in their camp, and were commanded by a son of the Emperor of Morocco. The mountain tribes again stood the French in good stead, for they descended on the flying army and murdered and plundered them as they passed, regardless of the fact that they were their own army and own countrymen.

On the 1st of September 1844, the Emperor of Morocco made overtures for peace, which was finally settled, particularly arranging that Abd-el-Kader should not for the future be allowed to harry the French from Morocco. The French marshal, to commemorate his victory, was created Duc d'Isly.

It should be noted that the English Government, though at first very suspicious of the designs of the French on Morocco, soon recovered their common sense. The French Government, in very temperate language, explained their position, and that Abd-el-Kader had been allowed to use Morocco as a recruiting ground and safe shelter for nearly two years, and that all they wished was to stop this perpetual border warfare. Lord Aberdeen, who was not only a personal friend of M. Guizot, the Prime Minister of France, but who also was Secretary of State for Foreign Affairs in England, was able to induce Sir Robert Peel, who was then head of the Government in England, to take a favourable view of the French side of the question. The result was that Mr. Drummond-Hay, the English Consul at Tangier, was personally sent to interview the Emperor of Morocco or his ministers, with a view of urging them to make peace, whilst the English fleet at Gibraltar was directed to make known to all the Moorish authorities at all the ports of that country that the English Government did not propose to interfere to save them from the French, as the demands of the latter were perfectly moderate and justifiable. There is but little doubt that this sensible arrangement on the part of the two European countries had a great effect in inducing the Emperor of Morocco to come

THE CONQUEST OF ALGERIA 179

to terms. If Abd-el-Kader had received the same hints from England earlier in his long war, much suffering to the Arab tribes and to the French soldiers might have been saved.

The Duc d'Isly sent out in October a small expedition from Dellys to bring some of the neighbouring Kabyles to order. It was attacked by these hardy mountaineers, and lost some 193 killed and wounded on the 17th of that month. He immediately repaired to Dellys with some 2,000 more men, and moved out and thoroughly broke up this party of Kabyles.

CHAPTER XIX

AN incident in the beginning of 1845 recalls some of the cases of the capture of British forts in America by the redskins in the eighteenth century. In January a band of Mahomedan pilgrims approached a small French fort in the south of Oran, and attempted to enter it. They appeared peaceably disposed, and were chanting religious hymns. As the door-keeper objected to their entering they killed him, and as the garrison rushed out to see what was happening, they killed them in turn, as naturally the men had no arms in their hands. Fortunately, the French soldiers ran back, obtained arms, and, as some intelligent person had shut the gates behind them, fifty-eight pilgrims were killed. There were no wounded Arabs on this occasion, and six French were killed and twenty-six wounded.

It showed how little the natives could be depended upon to keep the peace.

It will be remembered that the American Indians obtained admission to the British forts whilst playing a game of lacrosse, and in most cases were by this treacherous conduct able to capture the forts.

In the early part of the year 1845 the French made two interesting expeditions into the south of Algeria, on to the very edge of the Sahara desert. Taking Daya as a depôt for stores and provisions, one

THE CONQUEST OF ALGERIA 181

column went south in April, passing the salt lake of Chott-el-Chergu, and then, going south-east, Stitten was reached. It was a little walled town, but was deserted; also Rassoul and Brezina were visited. These were local markets, &c., for the nomad tribes of the desert, and it was a means of getting into touch with them. Unfortunately the inhabitants fled, and the French blew up the fortifications and retired. One rather pathetic incident is recorded. The French were approaching Brezina through a series of hills when an Arab came forward and offered to show them the best way, and led them in a circle back to the place he originally joined them at. It was found that he had purposely led them astray in order to give his townsmen time to escape. The French blew his brains out, but the devoted fellow had gained the necessary time for his friends to leave the town. The other expedition was a small affair near the Lake of Zahrez.

An insurrection now broke out in the hills on the borders of the provinces of Algiers and Oran. A saint arrived from Morocco called by the natives Bou Maza. He was able to gather some fanatics round him, and proceeded to murder some chiefs who were more or less friendly to the French. The whole country, barely settled, was soon in an uproar. A small fort was surprised and nearly captured, but the garrison rushed into the blockhouse and held out. The natives caught and cruelly killed before the eyes of the garrison a young girl, the daughter of a settler. A convoy was attacked and lost fifty-seven killed and wounded. Luckily, some of the tribes remained loyal and attacked Bou Maza, and after this fight 400 dead bodies of the enemy remained on the field. This rather ended Bou Maza's career, and he disappeared for the time being.

In June 1845 Colonel Pélissier led an expedition against some revolted tribes, who retired into caverns, which were well supplied with food and water. In reply to a summons to surrender, the natives fired on the messengers. The French then lowered fascines over the rocks against the mouths of the caves, and set fire to the pile of brushwood. This heap burnt during one night. Next day a further summons was sent, but was again received with contempt. More brushwood was piled on the fires, and a light breeze blew the smoke and sparks down one mouth of a cave and out at the other. The fugitives' stuff inside caught fire, and in the morning a few men came out and surrendered. The remainder, men, women, and children, had been suffocated: 500 bodies were found inside. Colonel Pélissier in reporting the matter used words to the effect that these sort of operations have to be done when necessary, but he prayed that God would never lay the necessity on him again.

A most excellent account of this unfortunate affair is given by Sir Lambert Playfair, who mentions that it is the account of a Spanish officer who was present, and it is probably fairly unbiassed.

'In June Colonel Pélissier pursued a body of rebels, who took refuge in some immense caves situated in a deep ravine between two hills. The Spanish officer says as follows:—" On the 18th (of June) the column of Colonel Pélissier left early to besiege the famous grotto or cavern which we had observed the day before situated on the bank of the Oued Frichih. After having sent chasseurs in front of the most accessible openings of El Kantara (the ravine above mentioned), the troops commenced to cut wood and to collect straw to light a fire on the west side, and thus oblige the Arabs to surrender, as any other means of attack would have been most sanguinary and probably fruitless. At 10 a.m. they commenced to throw the faggots from the counterfort of El Kantara, but the fire did not declare itself before noon. During the evening our tirailleurs approached nearer and shut in the openings of the cave. Nevertheless one of the Arabs succeeded in escaping from the east side, and seven others gained the banks of the stream, where they obtained a supply of water in their leathern vessels. At 1 p.m. the soldiers commenced to throw faggots at the eastern opening, which this time took fire before the two openings of the other side, and by a singular circumstance the wind blew both the flames and the smoke into the interior without almost any escaping outside, so that the soldiers were able to push the faggots into the openings of the cavern as into a furnace. It is impossible to describe the violence of the fire: the flame rose above the top of El Kantara (more than 180 feet high), and dense masses of smoke swept like a whirlwind before the entrance of the cavern. They continued to supply the fire all night, and only ceased at daybreak. But then the problem was solved: no further noise was heard. At 4.30 a.m. I went towards the cave with two officers of engineers, an officer of artillery, and a detachment of fifty or sixty men of their corps. At the entrance were found dead animals, already in a state of putrefaction; the door was reached through a mass of cinders and dust a foot in depth, and then we penetrated into a great cavity of about thirty paces in length. Nothing can give an idea of the horrible spectacle which presented itself in the cavern. All the bodies were naked, in positions which indicated the convulsions which they had suffered before death. What caused most horror was to see infants at the breast lying amongst the debris of sheep, sacks of beans, &c. The number of corpses amounted to 800 or 1,000. The colonel would not believe our report, and sent other soldiers to count the dead. They took about 600 out of the cave, without counting those ' entassés les uns sur les autres comme une sorte de bouillie humaine ' and the infants at the breast, who were nearly all concealed below the clothes of their mothers. The colonel testified all the horror which he felt at this frightful spectacle, and principally dreaded the attacks of the journals which could not fail to criticise so deplorable an act." '

Sir Lambert Playfair adds : ' It is not fair to quote this without quoting also the justification of the act which appeared in the Akhbar.

' In order that the public may be able to appreciate these sad events it ought to understand how important it was " pour la politique et pour l'humanité " to destroy the confidence which the population of the Dahra, and of many other places, had in the caves. . . . Colonel Pélissier invested them ; an operation which cost several lives—Arabs and French. When the investment was complete, he tried to parley with them by means of the Arabs in his camp; they fired on his *parlementaires*, and one of them was killed, nevertheless, by persistence, he succeeded in opening negotiations, which lasted all day ; without result.

THE CONQUEST OF ALGERIA 185

'The Oulad Riah always replied, "Let the French camp retire; we shall come out and submit ourselves." It was in vain that repeated promises were made to respect their persons and property, to consider none prisoners of war; but only to disarm them. From time to time they were informed that combustibles were collected, and that they should be warmed if they did not finish. Delay succeeded delay till the night arrived.'

After passing in review the probable consequences of retiring from the attack, the narrative continues, 'He decided on employing the means which had been recommended to him by the Governor-General'—with what success we have already seen. 'The caves are still (A.D. 1895) exactly in the condition in which they were then left, and no Arab can be induced to enter them.'

This incident has been made much of, and has been much used as showing how cruelly the French made war against the natives. War is cruel. The natives had the opportunity of surrendering. They declined to do so, and on them any blame for the matter must rest.

This severity had a good effect, and many rebels came to terms. In July a small expedition had to be sent from Dellys to check the insolence of the Kabyles, but there was no fighting to speak of.

Abd-el-Kader seized this favourable opportunity to make himself obnoxious. Raiding into the south of the province of Oran, he moved rapidly about with his cavalry, marching sixty miles a day. The French replied by making a road from Sebdou to Daya, Saida, and Tiaret, on which four towns they based their flying columns that they employed to keep the Emir away from the friendly tribes. Bou Maza suddenly reappeared and commenced murdering friendly natives towards the east.

He grew so strong that on the 23rd of September 1845 he attacked a French column and killed and wounded some eighty-two soldiers, and fighting went on for a week round it.

Strangely enough, Bou Maza was rather a weakness to Abd-el-Kader, as the natives, though quite willing to rise against the French, were rather doubtful which particular leader to follow.

Two unfortunate occurrences now took place which greatly raised the hopes of the Arabs. Abd-el-Kader, feeling that something must be done to regain some of his influence with the tribes, moved up to some mountains forty miles or so to the south-east of the new town of Nemours. The friendly Arabs called for help, and the colonel commanding at Nemours, de Montagnac, took with him some 425 men and went to their help on the 21st of September. His column was divided into two parts on the 23rd, and he and most of his men were killed after a desperate resistance. Some eighty men took refuge in a small mosque or tomb, and maintained a good fight. The Emir withdrew, leaving them blockaded by the Kabyles. After a three days' siege, being without water, these brave men broke out, carrying their wounded, and fought their way back towards Nemours. Some three miles from the place they found a stream, and the men then broke their ranks, despite the officer's commands, and rushed to the water. The enemy then shot most of them down, but some twelve were able to reach the town. A very brave act was done on this occasion. Abd-el-Kader sent up a French officer, who had been wounded and made prisoner, to summon the garrison, promising him his life if he obtained the surrender of the garrison, but that if they refused to surrender he would be beheaded. He promptly went up, told the garrison the conditions, and adjured them to fight to a finish, and went back and was duly murdered by the orders of the Emir. This hero's name was Dutertre. Acts like this justify almost any cruelty practised by the French, if indeed they ever committed any cruel acts unnecessarily. The second event was the disgraceful surrender without fighting of some 200 men under the command of an old lieutenant. This unfortunate man lost his head, and on the sight of the Arabs advancing, at once went forward and surrendered his force, which was a party marching from Tlemcen to reinforce the garrison of d'Ain Temouchent.

Not unnaturally, the whole place was in a ferment. Some tribes fled to Morocco, others blockaded the French ports, some of the depôts of provisions were burnt.

A French column 5,000 strong marched to where the fight had taken place when Colonel de Montagnac had been killed. There they found the tribes ready to receive them, supported by Abd-el-Kader. A sharp fight ensued, Abd-el-Kader fled, and his allies made submission to the French. The Emir then doubled back to the east and tried to carry Mascara, but found it well held, still the whole country was now up in arms and at his back. Troops were, however, poured in from France, raising the numbers of French troops in the country to over 100,000. The rebels became so bold that they tried to storm the town of Mostaganem on the 18th of October, but were repulsed.

Marshal Bugeaud moved out by Tiaret on the 24th of October with some 4,000 men. He executed a raid with his native horsemen under General Jusuf, of sixty miles from his camp, upon an unfriendly tribe, killed 300 men, and took all their flocks. Eleven other French columns were doing likewise, so that the rebels were in a sore strait. On the 21st of November Abd-el-Kader, who had remained hidden, suddenly raided a friendly Arab tribe. At once Marshal Bugeaud put eighteen columns in motion to catch him. Up and down this vast country went Abd-el-Kader with his flocks and fighting men, and after him the French. Not until the 23rd of December did they catch him up. Then after a short engagement he slipped away again, and the chase was resumed. Bou Maza now came in and made submission to Abd-el-Kader, and supported him with all his followers. Abd-el-Kader still led his pursuers a dance, and no wonder: when necessary he marched some 135 miles in the twenty-four hours. The Emir now tried to break through to get into the mountains between the province of Algiers and the province of Constantine, with a view of raising their Kabyle inhabitants. The last two battalions garrisoning Algiers itself boldly marched out and went to hold the passes in the neighbouring hills. An Arab camp was surprised on the 7th of February 1846, and Abd-el-Kader, who was sleeping in it, barely escaped with the loss of all his baggage. He managed to get into the mountain range of Djurdjura, south of Dellys. Marshal Bugeaud hunted him out at the end of February. Moving south, Abd-el-Kader fell upon a friendly tribe and plundered them, after a march of 120 miles in the twenty-four hours. Moving on more slowly with his plunder, a French column came up with him, and, after killing seventy of his men, picked up flocks and herds almost too numerous to count. This success was on the 7th of March. On the 13th General Jusuf fell upon the Emir's encampment, took all his baggage, and chased him south again. News now came in that some 280 French prisoners in Abd-el-Kader's camp in Morocco had been murdered. Besides the 200 men surrendered near Tlemcen, others had been picked up wounded. Unfortunately there is too much reason to think that the Emir gave the order for this massacre. One only of this party escaped. He was a trumpeter, and was taken by the Moors, who found him wounded and naked, to the French post at Lalla Maghnia, where he was ransomed. On the 3rd of July 1846 Abd-el-Kader crossed back into Morocco, after seven months of a chase during which he had lost almost all his adherents, but had given the French almost unheard-of trouble.

Whilst Abd-el-Kader was running up and down the country, all sorts of people started up as leaders of the rebels against the French. One person arrived from Morocco, giving out that he was our Saviour. He was attended by some 2,000 followers, and he had warned them that no arms need be taken by them, as he was able to cover the ground with French corpses at his will. Unfortunately for him, on attempting to enter Tlemcen, the spell did not work, and a squadron of hussars soon had his mob of disciples flying for their lives. The province of Constantine was fairly peaceable at this time, but a rebel tribe, egged on by a force from Tunis, fell upon a convoy of sick, marching for Boné, guarded by five native soldiers only. All these unfortunate men were killed excepting one of the escort. The chief of the revolted tribe appeared in the French camp and asked permission to lead the party to avenge this attack, as he said such conduct was not suitable to brave men. The tribe was cornered in the mountains, and were either killed by the French or driven over the precipices, whilst the forces from Tunis were met by the French cavalry, defeated, and chased for over twenty miles with great slaughter.

On the 23rd of November 1846, Abd-el-Kader sent eleven prisoners, who were still with him, to Melilla, where they were ransomed by a Spanish ship sent by the French. Amongst the eleven was the officer who had surrendered the 200 men some twelve months before. He was tried and condemned to death, but his sentence was remitted. The prisoners brought letters from the Emir to the French king and to Marshal Soult, desiring peace, but the letters were couched in a high tone, as from equal to equal. Marshal Bugeaud, after reading the letters, sent a message to the Emir to the effect that if he had sent the prisoners without ransom he would have returned him three for one, but after having so cruelly slaughtered the defenceless prisoners in his hands, he had no feelings for him but of indignation at his barbarity.

In the beginning of 1847, Bou Maza and another noted warrior of Abd-el-Kader, Ben Salem, surrendered to the French. Bou Maza was still regarded as a saint, and though a prisoner was followed by crowds of natives who thought themselves happy to be allowed to kiss his garment. In the beginning of May

THE CONQUEST OF ALGERIA 191

1847, a French column went as far south as Moghar, Tahtani, and all the neighbouring towns. There was practically no fighting in this march. Marshal Bugeaud was most anxious to be permitted to take a force into Morocco to root out once for all the last stronghold of Abd-el-Kader. The French Government objected to this expedition, and instead complained to the Moorish Government of the abuse of their territory by the Emir. In the meantime Marshal Bugeaud determined to bring the tribes of Grande Kabylie into subjection to the French. On the 13th of May 1847 he led some 7,000 men into the mountains from Bordj Bouira, whilst another column under General Bedeau, numbering 6,000 men, moved into the same district from Setif. There was some hard fighting, but the tribes attacked, after two days' fighting, made their peace, whilst other clans bided their time to fight against the French.

In the beginning of June 1847, Marshal Bugeaud resigned the command in Algeria and returned to France. He died there two years later of cholera. A fine, rough soldier, who made few enemies; France owes him much, and so does Algeria. General Bedeau took over the governor-generalship of Algeria, but on the 11th of September 1847 the Duc d'Aumale succeeded him.

The Moorish Government, pressed by the French consul at Tangier, decided to take steps to make Abd-el-Kader cease from his evil ways, and sent one of their chiefs with 2,500 men to take him prisoner. This chief called upon the Kabyles to support him, but they politely intimated that they proposed to remain neutral at present, but when they found which side was the stronger they would help that side. Whilst the Moorish force remained encamped, uncertain what to do, Abd-el-Kader rallied his followers and made a night march on the Moorish camp. He at once carried it and shot the chief in charge, but did not let his men pursue the flying Moors, professing great respect for the authority of the Emperor of Morocco. Unfortunately for the Emir the emperor was furious, and refused to be pacified. He commenced the campaign against Abd-el-Kader by striking at one of the immigrant tribes who favoured the Emir. They wished to migrate back again into Algeria, but the Moors did not wish to let them go, as they numbered 10,000 souls, from which they could draw 2,000 horsemen for fighting. This tribe was surrounded, and after three days' hard fighting all the men were killed, the women and flocks being handed over to the neighbouring tribes who had assisted at the massacre. Then the Kabyles, who had assisted the Emir when he had proved the stronger, were visited and overwhelmed, and finally it became the turn of Abd-el-Kader himself.

40,000, more or less regular, troops were led against him by two sons of the emperor. The country also rose against him. He took his stand on a river called Moulouia, which runs into the Isly, but decided to attack the Moors. He marched up on the night of the 11th of December 1847 for this purpose, bringing with him four horses loaded with tarred faggots. These poor brutes were to be set on fire and turned loose in the Moorish camps, with a view of setting all the tents on fire. However, the Moors found out from deserters what was happening, and moved out of their camps, leaving the tents standing. Thus when Abd-el-Kader

THE CONQUEST OF ALGERIA 193

entered with his three thousand men he found the place empty, but as day broke was assailed on all sides by the numerous enemy. The French just over the border watched the fight with a strong force, and kept sending ammunition to the Moors. Abd-el-Kader, after a magnificent fight of some days, on the 21st of December 1847 was swept over the border into Algeria, and, directing his following to surrender to the French, turned his horse's head south and headed for the Sahara. The French had every place and pass picqueted, and at 2 a.m. on the 22nd of December Abd-el-Kader was brought to a stand by a French outpost, in a pass. He asked permission to surrender. He demanded that he should be permitted to go to Alexandria or to Saint Jean d'Acre to live, and that all his goods should be guaranteed to him. General Lamoricière, who commanded the French troops in the province of Oran, acceded to all his requests, and on the 23rd of December 1847 Abd-el-Kader surrendered himself to the French at nine o'clock in the morning, at the little Mosque of Sidi Brahim, where in 1845 the 80 French had so gallantly fought against the overwhelming numbers of the Emir's army. His followers had already been received by the French to the number of 6,000 souls. The Duc d'Aumale arrived at Nemours that morning and confirmed the promise made to Abd-el-Kader, and had a very interesting conversation with him in the barrack there that evening. On the 24th of December he was sent to Toulon. It was only on that evening that the Emir mentioned that he was slightly wounded and asked for a surgeon. The Emir was retained in captivity in France until 1852. This has been advanced as an act of bad faith by France, but it was probably the best that could be done with him. If he had been handed over to the Khedive of Egypt or to the Turks at Acre he would only have been used as a pawn in the political game, or he might also have had convulsions after an interview with the Sultan or Khedive, as the last Dey of Algiers had, and have died in consequence. Such things used to happen. The fall of Abd-el-Kader had a great effect on the native mind, and peace reigned throughout Algeria in the beginning of 1848.

On the 3rd of March 1848 the Duc d'Aumale handed over the government to General Changarnier, as the revolution in Paris had driven his father from the throne and a republic had been established, and the French Republican Government had ordered him to withdraw.

CHAPTER XX

GENERAL CHANGARNIER was relieved of his government by the arrival of General Cavaignac from France on the 10th of March. General Changarnier again succeeded him on the 11th of May, and was himself superseded by General Marey on the 22nd of June, who was followed on the 22nd of September by General Charon, who ruled for two years. The Arabs did not understand this rapid succession of governors, and in a short time refused to pay the taxes. They were, however, collected by a column under General Marey, with a heavy fine added thereto for expenses. An expedition, led by Colonel Canrobert in the province of Constantine, pressed the rebels so hard in the mountains of l'Aurès, that on the 5th of June the late Bey of Constantine, Ahmed, surrendered to the column. In September 1848 there was some fighting with the Kabyles in the northern part of the province of Constantine, but, on the whole, the year was most peaceable.

In 1849, for some unknown reason, many of the tribes became restless, General Pèlissier led a column from Mascara, and ordered another out from Tlemcen under General MacMahon, both about 2,000 strong. These columns marched south to the borders of the desert, and took various fortified towns there, including Moghar-Tahtani before mentioned and others.

Where any violence had been used by the inhabitants to the natives with leanings towards the French, the palm trees were cut down and the walls blown up, otherwise little damage was done. Four columns also moved about the south of the province of Algiers, and the tribes gradually settled down again.

In the east still further trouble occurred in May 1849, but two columns working, one from Bougie and the other from Setif, brought peace or something like it to that part of the world; still, the Kabyles were no mean foes. For instance, on the 19th of May, the French lost 116 killed and wounded, whilst the Kabyles brought over 10,000 men armed with muskets into the field. A little later Colonel Canrobert took out some columns and had some hard fighting in the Djurdjura range of mountains. His heaviest loss was 42 killed and wounded in one day; the enemy must have lost heavily too, because the French tactics were to drive the natives into the villages from the hills and then overwhelm the villages with shell fire, and it succeeded very well.

In June 1849 a small revolt was raised in some oases south-west of Biskra. Zaatcha was the name of the chief town. It lay in a small forest of palm trees, through which forest there were few paths, and it was surrounded by a wet ditch twenty feet wide and too deep to be crossed by wading. Inside the ditch were thick walls loopholed for musketry, and inside that again were many houses having slits for windows most suitable for defence. The origin of the outbreak was the raising of the tax on the date trees from 25 to 40 centimes per tree. An Arab named Bou Ziane headed the revolt. A French lieutenant

THE CONQUEST OF ALGERIA 197

passing with seven men, heard that he was likely to give trouble, and tried to take him away prisoner, but the people rose and rescued him. Bou Ziane had lived an adventurous career, and for a time ruled his town for Abd-el-Kader, though he was of very low origin, having been a 'bhesti' or water-carrier in Algiers in 1833.

There was some delay in getting troops to Zaatcha, owing to the colonel in charge of the district being on an expedition. By the 16th of July, however, some 1,700 men were brought to Zaatcha. The surrounding small oases made their submission, but the chief offender remained defiant. Bou Ziane had meantime got a respectable garrison together, strengthened by parties from 'l'Aurés' mountains. The French tried to carry the place by assault, and launched their two columns about three o'clock in the afternoon; they fought their way to the walls and were there brought up, first by the unfordable ditch and then by the walls. The ditch was filled up with fascines, and a gun was brought up to batter down the wall, but at the ninth discharge the trail broke and the walls remained intact, as the shells appeared to bury themselves in the walls without causing much damage. The losses were 148 killed and wounded. The French remained on the ground for three days, and then retreated towards Biskra. Naturally, the whole of the tribes in the vicinity thought this a favourable time to rise; 5,000 Kabyles under some Moorish saint marched boldly on Biskra. The colonel in charge moved out at once on the 17th of September 1849, and attacked them with 400 regulars and 200 Arab horse. The Kabyles were routed and fled, leaving 200 men dead on the field. The French lost 14 killed and wounded, including the colonel in command, who was named Saint-Germain. He was killed early in the day, bravely leading the attack.

The French were greatly delayed in their preparations to retake Zaatcha by the outbreak of cholera. More than half their men were down with it. However, they sent columns through the neighbouring country to give the volunteers in the garrison of Zaatcha good reasons to wish to return to their own villages; and sent a column from Constantine some 4,500 strong on the 24th of September. This column arrived at Zaatcha on the 7th of October, bringing three siege mortars besides other guns, and many engineers for siegework. The African Light Infantry tried to clear the gardens, but were driven back, and lost 71 killed and wounded. A large number of the wounded were seized by the women of Zaatcha and tortured to death before the eyes of their comrades. During the night following some siege batteries were established less than 150 yards from the wall, but the palm trees were so numerous that the round shot could not reach the wall. The French lost 30 killed and wounded on the 8th, in a reconnaissance undertaken by Major Bourbaki to clear their left flank. During that night the palm trees were cut down by working parties of the infantry, and the batteries were advanced to within 100 yards of the enemy's works. Finding, however, that their artillery was not powerful enough to break down the walls, the French decided to work forward by sap. On the 12th of October reinforcements arrived for the French to the number of 1,650.

THE CONQUEST OF ALGERIA 199

The saps were pushed closer during a week and then the guns were brought close up to the walls, and these were breached at the angles. To fill up the ditch fascines were used, and when these failed, bricks were taken from the ruins of the suburbs and passed from hand to hand by a chain of infantrymen, and thus the ditch was made passable. On the 20th of October two storming columns were sent against the breaches; and the French did not make the usual English mistake of sending twenty men to do a thousand men's work and then grumbling at them if they should be unsuccessful, for the columns numbered respectively 1,300 and 750, whilst all the mounted men were sent under Major Bourbaki to patrol the borders of the oasis and to prevent assistance arriving from the neighbouring tribes. Both attacks, however, were repulsed. In one, a part of the tottering wall fell and crushed 11 men, 54 others were killed and wounded by the enemy's fire; whilst in the other assaulting column 104 fell, including the senior officers. The assault was most daringly conducted by the French, for finding the breach too steep to be climbed, they quietly lay down in the open and fired at the Arab loopholes, whilst the engineers vainly strove to undermine the walls. Finally, the columns fell back followed by the exulting Arabs; but they were easily driven within their walls again. More reinforcements were sent for to Constantine, also a demand for more siege guns and food. At the same time 600 invalids were sent to Biskra, for dysentery was very prevalent in the French camp. Whilst waiting reinforcements the French proceeded to cut down more palm trees. This drew the Arabs out of the town and they fiercely assaulted the French working parties, and only after hard fighting were driven back; the French lost 29 men in this action.

In the meantime some 1,500 of the Arabs from the Sahara came to the assistance of their co-religionists in distress; they were defeated after a short fight by some 400 French, with two mountain guns. Whilst this fight was going on, Bou Ziane, like the good leader he was, led a sally and set fire to the fascines in the French batteries. On the 5th of November, 100 natives dashed out of the town armed with torches, and again set fire to anything that would burn in the French trenches. Some 2,000 men came in from Setif and from Constantine by the 15th of November 1849, with two 12-pounders and with many captured flocks of sheep and a large convoy. Unfortunately cholera came with them; one detachment alone lost 120 men from it whilst on the march. The first use made of these reinforcements was to make a night march to attack the nomad tribes who hung threateningly on the borders of the oasis. Their camp was attacked at daybreak and 200 men killed, whilst besides the whole of the camp the French captured 1,800 camels and 15,000 sheep. Next day these tribes made their submission to the French. Meanwhile the besieged bravely attacked the trenches again, and by clever manipulation of the water flooded one series of trenches, causing great discomfort to the besiegers. A third breach was now made in the walls, and on the 26th of November a new assault was carried out. Three columns were employed: the first party was 800 strong, the second 950, and the third 880. Each column was preceded by a party of engineers, and two mountain guns came behind to be used as should be found most necessary. 2,200 men were sent out to cut off the retreat of the defenders and to prevent, as before, succour from reaching them. The night before this assault, Zaatcha was summoned for the last time, but proudly refused to surrender. The signal was given at seven o'clock in the morning, and by nine o'clock the three columns met in the square in the centre of the town. Each house, however, was a small fortress, and now had to be taken in succession by separate assault. The mountain guns were used for this, and when they failed, powder bags were piled against the walls, and thus gaps were blown in them, and then each house was rushed and the garrison slaughtered. Bou Ziane was now made prisoner. He came out of a house, wounded in the leg, leaning on one of his men, and surrendered, saying simply, 'I am Bou Ziane.' The French general in charge sent an order to his captors to have him shot at once. He had been taken prisoner by the Zouaves. These gallant men disliked shooting a man in cold blood, especially one who had made such a gallant fight for his own hearth and home as Bou Ziane, and they sent a second time for instructions. The order was sternly repeated and had to be complied with. On hearing his fate the Arab chief with quiet dignity said, 'You have proved the stronger. God only is great! His will be done.' The commander of the Zouaves reluctantly gave the order to four of his men that, on a certain signal being given, they should shoot the wounded man. He then went up to Bou Ziane, who was praying in the Arab style, and seizing him by the hand forced him to rise and led him to a wall. As he turned away he gave the signal, the four Zouaves fired together, and Bou Ziane fell dead. A natural feeling of sympathy is excited for this brave man only fighting for his country. Yet it must be admitted that those who go to war are likely to be killed; and he took his chance, and fate was against him.

The women of the town had cruelly murdered as many of the French wounded as they had been able to lay their hands upon, and it is greatly to be feared that many of them perished on this day. In any case every man was butchered, not one escaped; 800 corpses were counted lying upon the ruins, the remainder were under them.

The French lost in the assault 218 men. Their total loss during the siege, including sickness, was 165 killed and 790 wounded. Having utterly destroyed the town and cut down all the palm-trees, the troops moved back to Biskra on the 28th of November, leaving a howling wilderness behind them.

Truly a dreadful act: yet the whole was probably necessary to bring the surrounding tribes to reason. More lenient treatment would have been ascribed to weakness, and more bloodshed would have been the result.

CHAPTER XXI

ON the 6th of January 1850 the French were again in the field, having been defied by some small villages in the l'Aurès range. On arrival they found that the three villages to be taken were on a rocky crag, to which the only access was by steps or ledges of rock, each ledge being guarded by a solidly built stone tower. Three columns surrounded these villages, named Nara, and carried them in two hours; the defenders fled into the plain, but were caught by the cavalry and destroyed. Another expedition had to be sent in May from Setif towards Bougie, owing to an insurrection amongst the Kabyles. Here again fortune favoured the French, and they were able to drive their native enemies off the field, leaving over 200 dead behind them. The chief loss of the French in this affair was that of their General, de Barral, mortally wounded.

In November 1850, General d'Hautpoul became Governor-General of Algeria, and found the country perfectly quiet. In May 1851 the French decided to remove the passive blockade kept up by the Kabyles on Djidjelli. There were various reasons for this, but of late the Kabyles had become so insolent that they had nearly killed the French Governor of Philippeville, who only escaped in a boat, and had carried out a demonstration against Bougie. Two columns were sent out, both from Mila; the first numbered 8,700 men, the other column was quite weak, being about 1,000 strong.

The 8,700 men moved towards Djidjelli, the smaller column towards Bougie. Leaving Mila on the 9th of May 1851, the column fought its way to Djidjelli, where it arrived on the 16th of May, much battered; in one day alone it lost 66 killed, whilst it brought in 270 wounded. The Kabyles could certainly fight well in their mountains. The other expedition had some heavy fighting in the mountains towards Bougie. It was reinforced, did good work, and finally had its hardest fight near Collo, where it was furiously attacked by the Kabyles, but beat them off. The enemy left 80 dead on the field, but that the fight was a hard one is shown by the French casualties occasioned in this combat, viz. 328. This engagement took place on the 15th of July 1851.

At the close of the year 1851 a rebellion broke out in the mountains towards the west of the province of Constantine. Some holy man or mullah appeared, and even the powerful tribe of the Flissa joined the rebellion. The French sent two columns into the district, one of which was 5,000 strong; they took by storm a small village, named Tizilt-Mahmoud. It had the reputation amongst the tribes of being impregnable, and the French found that all the neighbouring peoples had sent their treasures to this place for safe keeping. It was sacked and destroyed, and all hastened to make their submission. On the 11th of December 1851, General Randon arrived in Algeria as governor-general. A small expedition was sent from Setif in January 1852 to chastise the

THE CONQUEST OF ALGERIA 205

Kabyles, who had again been blockading Bougie. In February the French suffered a loss of 50 men overwhelmed in a snow-storm in the hills outside Bougie; 200 others had their feet frost-bitten. Such a storm had never been heard of before in Algeria. The party who suffered numbered some 1,500 men, and were engaged in road-making, being assisted by working parties from the various Kabyle tribes. In July, General MacMahon crossed the border into Tunis in pursuit of some tribe which had emigrated from Algeria into that country. These men used Tunis as a refuge, and are said to have raided into Algeria from thence. The French surprised them and killed 400 men, and then, seizing their flocks, returned into Algeria. In the west of the province of Oran the French had to cross the border and bring to terms a tribe in Morocco, which tribe also was raiding over the border into Algeria. After a month or so these warriors sued for peace. On the 21st of May 1852, yet another marabout or warrior saint appeared on the scene. He was named Mohammed ben Abdallah. He moved up from the southern desert with 2,500 mounted men, and was met by the Commandant of Biskra, who attacked him boldly with 160 cavalry and 700 irregular Arabs. The latter would not charge, but the French cavalry gained the day, single-handed, killing 150 natives and wounding the saint himself. The holy man disappeared for the time being, but reappeared in November, at the twin towns of Laghouat. This place possessed one stream of water over which the two towns quarrelled. Not unnaturally, Mohammed took the side of the town which was anti-French, which happened to be the northern one. Three thousand men were brought against it by General Pélissier. He sent in a flag of truce demanding the surrender of the place, but his messenger was beheaded, and he proceeded to make a breach in the wall, and then sent twelve companies of Zouaves to the assault. The place was taken at once; but the saint escaped. Yet another expedition was sent into the mountains between Setif and Phillippville in May 1853 : 10,000 men were sent into this most rocky and mountainous country in three columns; the mountaineers, however, were found to be in a peaceable mood and only came to make their submission. Towards the end of 1855 there was some trouble with the tribes of the Sahara, to the south of Laghouat. On the 29th of November 1855, some 2,500 of these natives were met and defeated by some tribes friendly to the French; over 1,000 muskets were picked up on the battle-field. All the fortified villages of that part of the world surrendered to the French immediately afterwards.

During this time the Crimean War was in progress, and some 26,000 troops, cavalry and infantry, were sent from Algeria to the seat of war. A new native regiment was easily raised of over 2,000 strong to proceed to the war, which was looked upon by the Arabs as a holy war against the Infidels, in support of the Sultan of Turkey. The French Army in Algeria was reduced to below 50,000 men; still, the whole country remained fairly peaceable. Still one expedition had to be undertaken against the Kabyles of the upper reaches of the River Sebaou. On the 4th of June 1854, some 6,500 troops entered these mountains; they reappeared again after hard fighting on the 6th of July.

THE CONQUEST OF ALGERIA 207

Their losses were some 900 men killed and wounded, but the Kabyles of that district sued for peace.

In September 1856 the Kabyles brought a visit of the French Army on their heads, having tried to overwhelm some other tribes which were friendly to the French. The governor-general replied to this menace by moving 15,000 troops into their country, many of which troops were returned soldiers from the Crimea. The scene of the combat was to the north-west of the Djebel Djurjura range. The fighting was short, for though these tribes could produce 30,000 men armed with muskets, yet the whole country was not engaged in the affair. In one attack the French lost 83 men, but the natives submitted themselves to the French on the 9th of October 1856.

And now the last part of Algeria still independent was to be conquered, Grande Kabylia, that mountainous district running from Dellys towards the east. It was inhabited by the Kabyles, as its name showed, and was so thickly peopled that the French had to acknowledge that it would be impossible to put any French colonists amongst them. These Kabyles, though not always actively hostile to the French, were easily excited to acts of war by the preaching of their Mahomedan priests. Even at the best of times they were a defiant, independent race, given to quarrelling amongst themselves, and to blockading the French seaports: not by open hostility, but by simply not allowing goods to pass from the country to the French nor from the French into the country.

The governor-general ordered two large depôts to be made; one at Tizi-ouzou, the other at Dra-el-Mizane. He assembled over 30,000 men in May

1857, and took the command himself. He divided his force into four divisions, and gave orders that the men should leave their knapsacks behind, taking only their shelter tents and food for forty-eight hours, besides their arms and ammunition. Leaving Tizi-ouzou on the 24th of May, the 25th and 26th were spent in desperate fighting with the Kabyles; 612 men were killed and wounded on the French side in this affair. The French then settled down in the country, greatly to the dismay of the Kabyles, and built a fort, large enough to hold four battalions, and also made a carriage road to it. The fort was named at first Fort Napoleon, but was afterwards renamed Fort National.

Directly opposite to Fort Napoleon, and about three miles from it on another mountain, stood a Kabyle village, called I-cheriden. Here the unsubmitted Kabyles took their post, and proceeded to fortify it according to the best of their lights. A division was sent against it on the 24th of June, and after twenty minutes of a cannonade, the place was stormed. The French lost 371 men in this affair.

The French columns moved up and down the country freely, and Grande Kabylia sued for peace everywhere. The last fighting occurred on the 11th of July 1857.

The debt that Europe owes to France for the conquest of this country has seldom been recognised. The Regency of Algiers was a curse to every weak Christian nation. As has been well said, ' Algiers was founded, like Rome, by a band of thieves or brigands; unlike Rome, however, which after 300 years was a settled state, and rapidly becoming the

THE CONQUEST OF ALGERIA

leader of the world, Algiers only remained a nest of thieves: if possible, worse than in the beginning, because grown more strong. England tried to settle the matter by a bombardment in 1816. In 1830 the Dey had become so insolent that he was braving the wrath of France. What the conquest cost France in blood and treasure will, perhaps, never be known. Following M. Rousset's figures, the French lost 23,787 in action. More than half the actions, however, have no losses attached to them, and in some cases he mentions that the losses really exceeded those reported. Look at the mortality amongst the French caused by fever alone! Take some instances. From the 1st of June to the 1st of November 1840, 4,200 French soldiers died of fever, and this went on, more or less, every summer. Again, at Miliana, in 1840, out of some 1,300 men of the garrison there, less than 100 were alive at the end of the year. What it must have cost to maintain the army alone in Algeria, sometimes over 100,000 strong, is surely a very large sum. Yet all this was done by France, at her own expense, and Europe reaps the benefit. But not Europe only. Surely it is better for the Arab and Kabyle tribes to dwell at peace under the French flag, than to be in a perpetual state of internal warfare, the strong always plundering and murdering the weak. Whatever motives France may have had originally to induce her to take this work in hand, the results have been good for all, and all who care for the advancement of civilisation must acknowledge her noble efforts for the good of the many peoples of Algeria.

APPENDIX

A SHORT summary of events which have taken place in Algeria since its conquest by the French may not be uninteresting to the casual reader.

From A.D. 1830 to A.D. 1857, with the possible exception of the early part of A.D. 1848, the French were always at war in some part of this large territory. This is not surprising when we remember that, although the Turks had held the country for some 300 years, yet they had always been in the same case as the French during the whole time, i.e. in a state of perpetual war; and again, the Turks had never succeeded in forcing their way permanently into the mountains inhabited by the Kabyles, and had thus really never conquered a large part of the country.

The French struggled on, at first in a feeble way after A.D. 1830, and then more and more strongly, until at length their army exceeded 100,000 men, and when large numbers of that army returned from the Crimean War, they sought out and gave the finishing stroke to that hornets' nest, Grande Kabylia, in A.D. 1857. From that time they and the natives both acknowledged that the conquest of Algeria was complete. The French settled down to improve their new territory by making roads and railways and artesian wells, &c.

In A.D. 1864, 1865, and 1869, there were small Arab rebellions in the south of Algeria, but of such a trivial nature that Sir Lambert Playfair does not notice them in his works on that country. In A.D. 1870 the disastrous war between Germany and France broke out in August, and the French troops were practically all withdrawn from Algeria to meet the German invaders. Besides this, many of the higher officials in the 'Bureau Arabe' (which managed native affairs in Algeria) quitted their posts to assist in the raising of the new levies in France, as many of them were experienced soldiers. The native troops also were sent to the front in France from Algeria, and behaved extremely well in action, especially at the battle of Worth on the 6th of August 1870, under Marshal MacMahon. The fact of sending them on active service in France had two satisfactory results. It first prevented any mutiny amongst the native troops, which might have occurred if the native army had not been removed to France, and the French were thus spared the danger of having a repetition of the Indian Mutiny on their hands at a critical moment. The second satisfactory result was that there was at first a marked feeling of sympathy amongst the natives for the French in their troubles, as the natives felt that their own friends and relations were being killed and wounded in the same national cause.

The great Arab chiefs, as a rule, were friendly to the cause of Napoleon the Third, and were distressed at his downfall, and their aristocratic ideas were upset at the idea of a republic. Various impolitic measures of the Provisional Government of France, under the hand of Gambetta, rather repelled them, such as the conferring of citizenship on all the Jewish inhabitants of the country. These people had always been looked upon with contempt by the Mahomedans, and the dignity of the latter was offended by this act of the Government.

In January 1871 an insurrection broke out at Souh Ahras, a town in the province of Constantine. It was headed by some irregular Arab horsemen in the pay of France, and they speedily drew with them their own neighbouring tribes and proceeded on a course of pillage and murder amongst the defenceless colonists scattered about on their farms. Some troops hurriedly sent from Boné broke the rebels up at once, and they escaped into Tunis. Abd-el-Kader's son also stirred up trouble, and yet a third revolt broke out near Philippeville, and the whole of the Sahara rose as one man and waged war cheerfully on one another, each asserting, in the Sahara at least, that he was fighting for the French, whilst he really was only stealing his neighbour's flocks for his own private benefit. The other two disturbances were easily quelled by a small column of French troops sent from Collo.

The small town of Tuggurt, some 130 miles from Biskra in the desert, was captured by the insurgents and the garrison murdered.

APPENDIX 213

This was the first place where the French had constructed an artesian well in 1856.

Peace was now signed by France with Germany, and veteran French troops were poured into the colony. This moment was seized by the great chiefs to revolt. The revolt was most cleverly carried on, despite its inopportune time of breaking out. Three chiefs were chosen to lead, of whom one was to rule and lead the Arabs or tribes of the plain and desert, another the mountaineers, whilst the third was to remain in Algiers and give the other two such information as he might be able to worm out of the French. It is not stated how the spoils were to be divided if these three had been successful; probably there would have been some bickering between them then. The first serious outbreak occurred some forty-five miles from Setif, near Constantine, whilst just previous to this five poor Europeans, working at road-making at the Portes de Fer, were murdered. Bougie was besieged. The whole of Kabylia was up. Many brave deeds were done by the unfortunate Christians so suddenly and so cruelly attacked. Whenever any place was taken, all the European males were invariably put to death. Naturally very few places were taken under such circumstances. At one little fort called Beni Mansour, some fifteen miles or so from the Portes de Fer, and on the Algiers side of them, the Kabyles brought up with much ceremony a cannon which had been captured from the Duc de Beaufort in 1664, when he was attacking Djidjelli. It bore the inscription: 'Anno Dei 1635.' 'Deos me aivet' ('Deus me adjuvet'), according to Sir Lambert Playfair. However, despite all attempts, the garrison held out even against this venerable piece of ordnance.

By August 1871 the insurrection was thoroughly crushed, and the revolted tribes who sued for peace were disarmed, condemned to pay a fine of £1,200,000, and, further, 250,000 acres of their most fertile lands were taken from them. These lands were handed over to French settlers from Alsace Lorraine, which two provinces had been ceded by France to Germany. Those inhabitants of these countries who wished to still remain French subjects were permitted to leave the country by the Germans, and were given free grants of land in Algeria by the French Government.

One rebel deserves special mention. He was named Mokrani, and was one of the three chiefs before mentioned as being in a conspiracy against the French. He had been well received in France previous to the war of 1870, and he had promised the French Governor-General that he would remain faithful to her so long as she was at war. He was an elderly man, and had helped France faithfully in many tribal frays, but he was bitterly opposed to the Jews. As he was deeply in debt there may have been personal reasons for this attitude.

So soon as peace was signed between France and Germany he sent in a formal declaration of war, and resigned his French offices and returned his Legion of Honour, and then permitted forty-eight hours to elapse before he entered on his operations—presumably to allow the isolated French families to escape. He fought his last fight, after a gallant campaign, at a place called Souflat, and seeing that all was lost save honour, he dismounted from his horse and led his men valiantly forward on foot against the French regulars, until a kindly Chassepot bullet struck him in the forehead and laid him low.

In May A.D. 1879 an insurrection broke out in l'Aurès mountains, which will be remembered as the refuge of Ahmed, the last Bey of Constantine, after the fall of his capital. It was raised, as so often happens in Mahomedan countries, through the preaching of a marabout. The rebels advanced boldly to meet the French, but the breech-loader, in the hands of the French infantry, was too much for them: 1,500 of them were driven in headlong rout before a few Frenchmen, leaving 400 dead on the field; 300 or 400 others were driven into the Sahara and died of thirst, whilst the marabout and some others fled to Tunis, and were handed over by the authorities there to the French, and they were duly tried by court-martial and executed.

In 1881 there was an outbreak amongst the Arabs on the borders of the Sahara, in the east of the province of Oran. Many Europeans were murdered, but the ferment subsided, and French columns moved up and down the country, but no engagements of any importance took place, and the leaders of the outbreak escaped.

There is but little doubt that insignificant tribal fights have

APPENDIX

taken place since then in the oases, but they have been of small consequence.

Attached is a list of the troops now maintained in Algeria. These troops are not colonial but metropolitan troops, and, combined with one division in Tunis, constitute the XIX Army Corps. In round numbers the whole amount to some 50,000 men. The cavalry is arranged in four brigades, and the infantry in four divisions.

The cavalry consist of six regiments of Chasseurs d'Afrique and four regiments of Spahis; the former are almost exclusively Frenchmen, and the latter are nominally Arabs and wear the Arab burnous and turban. Vacancies in the Spahis are sometimes filled by Frenchmen, who wear the fez instead of the turban.

The numbers according to the arms are roughly as follows, including Tunis :—

Four Cavalry Brigades . . .	5,600 sabres.
Four Infantry „ . . .	25,200 rifles.
(In Algeria).	
Two Infantry „ . . .	12,600 „
(In occupation of Tunis).	
Twenty-three batteries (120 guns)— fifteen Field Artillery and eight Fortress Batteries	5,000 men.
Engineers, A.S.C. Staff, and Intendance, &c.	4,000 „

XIX Army Corps, Algeria and Tunis

Division		Brigade		Regiment		Territorial Army
No.	Head-quarters	No.	Head-quarters	No.	Head-quarters	
Algiers divisi'n	Algiers	1st Inf. (Algeria)	Algiers	1st Zouaves 1st Algerian Tirailleurs 4th company Fusiliers de Discipline	Algiers Blida Aumale	Infantry — 4 battns. of Zouaves (1st to 4th).
		1st Cav. (Algeria)	Medea	1st Chasseurs d'Afrique 5th ,, ,, 1st Spahis	Blida Algiers Medea	Cavalry—5th squadron Chasseurs d'Afrique Artillery — 3 Fortress batteries of 11th battn. of Foot Artillery
		Non-Brigaded Troops		2nd battalion African Light Infantry 11th battn. Foot Artillery 14th, 17th, and 18th batts. 12th Artillery 26th battalion Engineers 11th, 12th, and 13th squadrons train	Laghouat Algiers Algiers Algiers Algiers	
Oran divisi'n	Oran	2nd Inf. (Algeria)	Oran	2nd Zouaves 2nd Algerian Tirailleurs	Oran Mostaganem	Zouaves — 4 battns. (6th to 9th)
		3rd Inf. (Algeria)	Mascara	1st Foreign Legion 2nd ,, ,,	Sidi-bel-Abbes Saida	Cav., 6th sqd. Chasseurs d'Afrique
		2nd Cav. (Algeria)	Tlemcen	2nd Chasseurs d'Afrique 6th ,, ,, 2nd Spahis	Tlemcen Mascara Sidi-bel-Abbes	
		Non-Brigaded Troops		1st battalion African Light Infantry 3rd company Fusiliers de Discipline 13th, 15th, and 16th batteries of 12th Artillery 4th coy. 19th battery Engineers	Le Kreider Mecheria Oran Oran	
Tunis divisi'n of occupation	Tunis	1st Inf. (Tunisia)	Tunis	4th Zouaves 3rd battalion African Light Infantry 5th battalion African Light Infantry	Tunis Le Kef Camp Servieres	Inf.—1 battalion Zouaves (15th)
		2nd Inf. (Tunisia)	Sousse	4th Algerian Tirailleurs 4th battalion African Light Infantry 1st co. Fusiliers de Discipline	Sousse Gabes Gafsa	
		Cav. Bde. (Tunisia)	Tunis	4th Chasseurs d'Afrique 4th Spahis	Tunis Sfax	

APPENDIX

XIX ARMY CORPS, ALGERIA AND TUNIS (*continued*)

Division		Brigade		Regiment		Territorial Army
No.	Head-quarters	No.	Head-quarters	No.	Head-quarters	
		Non-Brigaded Troops		3rd battn. Foot Artillery	Biserta	
				1st, 2nd, and 3rd batts. 6th Artillery	La Manouba	
				21st batt. 13th Artillery	Sousse	
				16th batt. ,, ,,	Biserta	
				17th batt. ,, ,,	Hamman Lif	
				Detachment 6th comp. Workmen	Tunis	
				26th battl. Engineers {	Tunis / Biserta	
Constantine divisi'n	Constantine	4th Inf. (Algeria)	Constantine	3rd Zouaves	Constantine	Infantry — 3 battalions of Zouaves (11th, 12th, and 13tb)
				3rd Algerian Tirailleurs	Constantine	
		3rd Cav. (Algeria)	Setif	3rd Chasseurs d'Afrique	Constantine	Cav. 3rd sqd. Chasseurs d' Afrique
				3rd Spahis	Batua	
		Non-Brigaded Troops		2nd co. Fus. de Discipli'e	Biskra	
				14th, 15th, & 18th batts. 13th Artillery	Constantine	
				4th coy. 12th battalion Engineers	Constantine	

www.ingramcontent.com/pod-product-compliance
Lightning Source LLC
Chambersburg PA
CBHW052050220426
43663CB00012B/2507